MW00439866

WISEWORDS FOR GOLFERS

WISE WORDS FOR GOLFERS

*A Dazzling Compendium of Quotes,
Anecdotes, and Gems of Wisdom from
the Royal and Ancient Game*

COMPILED AND EDITED BY
DALE CONCANNON

THOMAS DUNNE BOOKS
ST. MARTIN'S PRESS
NEW YORK

THOMAS DUNNE BOOKS
A Division of St. Martin's Press

www.stmartins.com

ISBN 0-312-27525-0

First published in Great Britain by Pavilion Books Limited

First U.S. Edition: June 2001

10 9 8 7 6 5 4 3 2 1

Contents

For my brother Carl

Introduction

What makes the game of golf so special? For those people fortunate enough to have escaped its clutches, the devotion it inspires from its followers must appear quite absurd. Certainly at times, all that physical effort and mental anguish must seem wildly disproportionate to the amount of pleasure it appears to bring. Indeed, most golfers would agree with this. After all, who knows what dizzy heights many of us could achieve if but a small fraction of the energy and finance we invested in the sport was directed towards a more sensible goal?

Golf is a game of temperament and character, offering unlimited potential for personal embarrassment and failure. Golfers do well to remember that bunkers are not moved during the night just to capture that wicked slice you picked up last week! And oak trees have not spent the last two hundred years growing solely with the intention of blocking your path to the green – no matter what you may think!

Winston Churchill once described it as 'hitting a small ball into an even smaller hole with weapons ill-designed for the purpose'. He was probably right. Yet it is overcoming these many challenges that makes the playing of it so rewarding. Over the years a vast body of writing has built up which far surpasses any other sport for sheer quality and quantity. And while many of the contributions to the literature of golf have fallen by the wayside over the years, others by comparison are wonderfully well written and often breathtaking in their insight. This, in essence, is what this book is all about.

Among the most comprehensive collections of golf writing ever gathered together in one book, with a varied mixture of comment, history and first-class golf writing, it offers an invaluable glimpse into the idiosyncratic nature of golf and those who play it. From advice on how to play the game to the trials of championship golf, each quotation reflects the abiding passion golfers have for their sport and in part, helps explain why golf is the wonderful game it is. There are revealing and entertaining insights from some of the finest writers and authors including Alistair Cooke, Mark Twain, Bernard Darwin and P. G. Wodehouse.

The book has twenty chapters, each dealing with a distinctive area of golf. These include 'The Exasperating Game of Golf', which details some of the elements which have so frustrated golfers over the years. A rich medley of extracts, comment and observation, it includes comments by such diverse writers as Bernard Darwin, former British Prime Minister Arthur Balfour and the legendary American amateur, Bobby Jones.

In 'A Royal and Very Ancient Game' the early history and development of the sport is highlighted with quotations that date back to the fifteenth century. In 'Championship Golf' the heart-thumping drama of tournament play is covered in depth. 'On Course' showcases some of the world's most famous golf courses, as well as individual holes, while 'Legends of the Game' features some of the greatest golfers of all time. The remaining chapters are a potpourri of interesting and varied items on, for example, the art of matchplay, women's golf, advice from the gurus, celebrity golf, caddying and putting.

It was decided at the outset that, in the search for likely material, no area would be out of bounds. Great effort has been made to strike a happy balance between the serious and the humorous, trivial and informative, old favourites and new. From the vast array of short stories, magazine articles, biographies, historical items, memoirs, humour and travelogues, the final selection depended on quality and interest.

Inevitably, some quotations will have been published in anthology form before. But I am proud to say this book also contains many items which have rarely seen the light of day. I hope that these, like many of the others, will become firm favourites in the future.

Finally, one of the great pleasures of editing a book like this is the opportunity to re-visit some old friends. With so many wonderful writers to choose from, I still find the descriptive work of Horace Hutchinson, Sir Walter Simpson and Garden G. Smith as fresh today as I did many years ago when first chancing upon them in my local library.

The same applies to the wonderful commentaries of that eighteenth-century chronicler, Tobias Smollett. His description of those Gentleman Golfers of Leith is as fresh today as it was when it was written. His subtle rebuke of their behaviour and how 'they never went to bed without having each the best part of a gallon of claret in his belly' offers a glorious insight into how the game of golf was enjoyed over two centuries ago.

Now, as I sit back and read it once more, those venerable old golfers with their whiskers and top hats seem to come alive on the page. I can picture the look of eager anticipation as each one tees up his feathery ball on a pinch of sand and sweeps it away down those ancient fairways. The glint of evening sun on his top hat, the joyful chatter as they stride purposefully down the fairway attended by a small posse of scruffy caddies. Surely this was golf at its very best.

The aim of this book is to celebrate that time and many others. I hope you have as much pleasure reading as I did putting it together.

DALE CONCANNON
BOURNEMOUTH, ENGLAND
JANUARY 2000

The Best Game
in the World

Golf keeps the heart young and the eyes clear.

ANDREW KIRKALDY, SCOTTISH PROFESSIONAL OF THE EARLY
1900s

Wherein do the charms of this game lie, that captivate youth,
and retain their hold till far on in life? It is a fine, open-air, athletic exercise, not violent, but bringing into play nearly all the
muscles of the body; while that exercise can be continued for
hours. It is a game of skill, needing mind and thought and
judgement, as well as a cunning hand. It is also a social game,
where one may go out with one friend or with three, as the case
may be, and enjoy mutual intercourse, mingled with an excitement which is very pleasing ... It never pails or grows stale, as
morning by morning the players appear at the teeing-ground
with as keen a relish as if they had not seen a club for a month.

JAMES BALFOUR, 1887

I have loved playing the game and practising it. Whether my
schedule for the following day called for a tournament round or

merely a trip to the practice tee, the prospect that there was going to be golf in it made me feel privileged and extremely happy. I couldn't wait for the sun to come up so that I could get out on the course again.

BEN HOGAN

[Golf] is visual; it has texture, it has emotions it has power.

BETTY JAMESON, FORMER AMERICAN LPGA STAR

Golf is deceptively simple, endlessly complicated. A child can play it well, and a grown man can never master it. Any single round of it is full and tantalizing, precise and unpredictable. It requires complete concentration and total relaxation. It satisfies the soul and frustrates the intellect. It is at the same time rewarding and maddening — and it is without doubt the greatest game mankind has ever invented.

ROBERT FORGAN, 1899

No inconvenient reminiscences of the ordinary workaday world, no intervals of weariness or monotony interrupt the pleasures of the game. And of what other recreation can this be said?

A. J. BALFOUR, *THE HUMOURS OF GOLF*, 1890

Golf in its own special nature of being brings nations together more than any other sport, it is a world-wide pastime.

ROBERT HARRIS, *SIXTY YEARS OF GOLF*, 1953

Golf may be ... a sophisticated game. At least, it is usually played with the outward appearance of great dignity. It is, nevertheless, a game of considerable passion, either of the explosive type, or that which burns inwardly and sears the soul.

BOBBY JONES

For the golfer, Nature loses her significance. Larks, the casts of worms, the buzzing of bees, and even children are hateful ... Rain comes to be regarded solely in its relation to the putting greens, the daisy is detested, botanical specimens are but 'hazards', twigs 'break clubs'. Winds cease to be east, south, west or north. They are ahead, behind, sideways. And the sky is dark, according to the state of the game.

SIR WALTER SIMPSON

Golf's lexicon of colourful words and phrases is its crowning achievement. For long after the urge of the ability to play the game leaves us, golf's joyful adjectives and modifiers, its splendid superlatives and unequalled accolades ring in my ear the waves of a familiar sound.

ROBERT BROWNING

The walking a golfer does is purposeful, and therefore never tiresome; but when five or six miles have been covered by a stout person, a trifle short of breath, and specially if the course be a good deal up and down hill, that player when the last hole has been made will be apt to conclude that he or she has been doing something. And if the score shows that the player has improved since the last game then the wholesome fatigue will be doubly grateful and the next golfing day be looked forward to with pleasurable anticipations.

JOHN GILMER SPEED, *THE LADIES JOURNAL*, 1894

On top of my interest in the game itself, I took a tremendous interest in the clubs and balls, particularly the latter. I had seen many changes in the golf ball, and I believe the great development in the game of golf is directly attributable to the wonderful strides made by the manufacturers in perfecting the ball and making the game a more pleasant one to play.

FRANCIS OUIMET

Golf: a game in which you claim the privileges of age, and retain the playthings of childhood.

SAMUEL JOHNSON, ENGLISH ESSAYIST

Beyond the fact that it is a limitless arena for the full play of human nature, there is no sure accounting for golf's fascination. Obviously yet mysteriously, it furnishes its devotees with an intense, many-sided, and abiding pleasure unlike that which any other form of recreation affords ... Perhaps it is nothing more than the best game man has ever devised.

HERBERT WARREN WIND

Golf is eminently a game of relaxation of mind if not of body. To the city man, worn out by want of business, or by too much business, it comes as a boon and a blessing, for it not only gives him the opportunity of obtaining fresh air and exercise, but it also brushes away the cobwebs from his over-tired brain.

S. MURE FERGUSSON, TOP BRITISH AMATEUR, 1914

The Sport of Kings, the pastime of the people, the game of the old and the young, golf can be played by all. All classes may mingle, all shapes and sizes may adapt themselves, the light-weight has an equal chance with the heaviest, all play on the same ground on equal footing. Golf has become International and Universal.

ROBERT HARRIS, *SIXTY YEARS OF GOLF*, 1953

When I came up, my ball was about three yards from the hole. Two putts made 99. I felt I was now really a golfer.

ARTHUR RAINSFORD, BRITISH WRITER, 1962

....

The satisfaction of knowing that you may depend upon your partner in every crisis of the game is exactly the feeling that gives quiet confidence and pleasure to the owner-driver of an Austin car.

A PROMOTIONAL ITEM FROM THE AUSTIN MOTOR COMPANY, 1934

....

The principal qualifications for the game are steady nerve and eye and good judgement and force with an added ability to avoid knolls and sand-pits which, in the technical terms of the Scotch game, are called hazards. It is not a game which would induce men of elegance to compete in, but those who have strong wind and good muscle may find it a splendid exercise for their abilities, and plenty of chance to emulate each other in skill and physical endeavour.

ALEXANDER MACFARLANE, *GLOBE-DEMOCRAT* NEWSPAPER, 1889

It hasn't stopped people playing golf. Some are even wearing smoke masks ...

SPOKESMAN FOR THE *NORTH FLORIDA PGA* ON THE FOREST FIRES WHICH RAVAGED THE DAYTONA BEACH AREA IN THE MID-1990S

The terrible thing about a missed shot in golf is that the thing is done, irrevocably, irretrievably. Perhaps that is why golf is so great a game; it is so much like the game of life. We don't have the shots over in either.

O. B. KEELER, AMERICAN SPORTSWRITER

Mr Jeston asked me if I would like a round at Sandwich ... We set off in his Armstrong-Siddeley immediately after lunch. The sun was hot. As we walked to the first tee of the first 'Championship' links I had ever seen ... ahead was sheer emerald of fairway, grey-green of rough and sand-hill. Above, the sky was starry with singing larks; there was a tiny shimmering breeze blowing into my face from Pegwell Bay. Three hours later I walked off the 18th green. To describe what had happened is impossible. I was in a dream come true before I had dreamed it. I had been, as it were, in a controlled ecstasy not aware that ecstasy existed, only a little aware that control had come from outside me. Let me put down the traces of this divine visitation; I did seventeen of the holes in five strokes each; one I did in four. Eighty-nine strokes. My fives at the bogey-fours were never less than commendable, my fives at the bogey-fives were exciting, sometimes magical triumphs. All the round long 'it was shining, it was lovely'. I was so light with joy

I could feel the grasses under my feet growing me taller, as they grew. There were tiny flowers and traces of rabbits and the scent of hot dry sand, dry sweet grass, and the bitter-sweet of salt – a tasty outdoor kitcheny sort of smell. I have often tried to write a poem about golf, but I have never been able to. This round was my poem of golf, perhaps that is the reason.

LETTER TO *GOLF MONTHLY*, FROM A GOLF ADDICT, 1923

I have played in a two-ball six-some, on the same side as an Irish Protestant parson from Cork and an average-adjuster – a profession, surely, of magnificent vagueness to the uninitiated. I cannot recollect who won. At Lindrick, that lovely course on the borders of three counties, I have partaken in a one-hole, one-club match with fourteen others, on a summer's evening, and the heavens were darkened with balls, as was the sun, so they say, with arrows at Marathon!

R. C. ROBERTSON-GLASGOW, *MORNING POST*

I am quite certain that there has never been a greater addition to the lighter side of civilization than that supplied by the game of golf.

A. J. BALFOUR, 1900

I don't know who he is, but he's good company.

BILLY CASPER, FORMER MASTERS CHAMPION, ON BEING PAIRED AT AUGUSTA WITH SPIDER MILLER, AMERICAN MID-AMATEUR CHAMPION, WHO ALSO HAPPENS TO OWN A BREWERY IN INDIANA, 1997

It was straight on the flag, and I wanted to shout, 'Cor, look at that.' I went hot and cold all at the same time and then it was all over.

NICK FALDO, THE EVENTUAL WINNER, ON HIS FIVE-IRON APPROACH TO THE 72ND GREEN DURING THE OPEN CHAMPIONSHIP AT MUIRFIELD, 1987

What's over there? A nudist colony?

LEE TREVINO, WONDERING WHY HIS THREE PARTNERS HAD DRIVEN INTO THE TREES ON ONE HOLE, 1970s

It is a curious thing about golf that those who play it enter an enclosed world with its own private language understood only by the initiated. If, like myself, you are not of that world, you can't enter into the fun, share the same jokes, etc. Perhaps, to twist the Stevenson line, lack of proficiency in golf is really the true sign of a misspent youth.

FRANK MUIR, BRITISH AUTHOR AND WIT

I hit some shots on the back nine that impressed even me!

PETER JACOBSON, AFTER HIS FINAL ROUND IN THE BRITISH OPEN CHAMPIONSHIP AT SANDWICH, 1986

Expert golf playing is an art, not a trade.

BOB HARLOW, RENOWNED GOLF PROMOTER, 1936

On the course, I learn about myself, the sport, the other competitors, nature, discipline and mind control. It is an enlightening experience.

MAMORU OSANAI, A LITTLE-KNOWN JAPANESE PROFESSIONAL WHO CLEARLY GETS A LOT MORE OUT OF PLAYING GOLF TOURNAMENTS THAN JUST PRIZE MONEY, 1999

Baseball is too strenuous for the person who does not play regularly. Many play until they reach 21. After that they quit the game as a regular form of exercise and pleasure, unless they go into the professional ranks. But golf is a game for all ages. The old as well as the young can play. It gives one as much fresh air as does baseball, and keeps one healthy without straining the muscles.

THE NEW YORK TIMES, 1915

In reality, there was never a more fascinating, nor a more healthful game invented than golf.

JOHN GILMER SPEED, THE LADIES JOURNAL, 1894

There is no reason, in the nature of things, why golf should not be begun as soon as one can walk, and continued as long as one can walk.

PETER CAVENDISH, FROM TEE TO GREEN, 1996

A champion is not a champion because he wins, but because of how he conducts himself.

DOUG SANDERS

Bobby Jones came as close to golfing perfection as it is possible to achieve. Remaining an amateur throughout his entire career, he competed against and consistently beat some of the greatest professionals the game has ever known. During his own lifetime and for over half a century since, Jones has been the yardstick against which all other great golfers are measured.

A.J. DALCONEN, *GOLF: THE HISTORY OF THE ROYAL & ANCIENT GAME*, 1995

....

One might as well attempt to describe the smoothness of the wind as to paint a clear picture of his swing.

GRANTLAND RICE, ON THE GOLF SWING OF BOBBY JONES

....

You can hear it but you can't see it!

Spectator at the 1997 Masters at Augusta, overheard describing a full-blooded Tiger Woods drive

He would not play any course twice in the same day. Why not? Because he was so accurate, that in his second round, his shots finished in the divot holes he had made in the morning, and that took the fun out of the game for him.

Henry Cotton, talking about six times British Open Champion, Harry Vardon

When your name is Zoeller, and so many things are done in alphabetical order, you expect to be last.

Fuzzy Zoeller, twice a Major winner

I just wanted to see what liberties I could take with the rough.

Jack Nicklaus, who deliberately missed the fairways in practice at the 1972 Open at Muirfield

I won't say my golf is bad; but if I started growing tomatoes, they'd come up sliced.

Miller Barber

I've played in Japan. Is that anywhere near Asia?

Fred Couples, asked if he had ever played golf in Asia

I wear black. I loved Westerns and the cowboys always looked good in black.

Gary Player, on his reasons for wearing black

I used to wade into the ponds on a little nine-hole Country Club that I grew up on. I wasn't old enough to play on it but I used to take the balls I found on the baseball field and there was this little guy who I used to fight all the time when I was four or five years old. He lived just across the neighbourhood so I used to take the balls and try and hit his house with them. When I got to about six or seven, I started to hit the windows. I was a little bigger than he was, but his dad was a lot bigger, so I quit.

JOHN DALY, EXPLAINING HOW HE GOT HIS START IN GOLF

Like a lot of fellows on the Senior Tour, I have a furniture problem — my chest has fallen into my drawers.

BILLY CASPER

Golf is a puzzle without an answer. I've played golf for forty years and I still haven't the slightest idea how to play.

GARY PLAYER

Here lies Arnie Palmer. He always went for the green.

MARK McCORMACK'S PROPOSED EPITAPH FOR HIS MOST FAMOUS CLIENT

That Daly fellow could knock the cap off your head at 200 yards with his two-iron.

GERALD MICKLEM, FORMER CAPTAIN OF THE R & A, TALKING ABOUT THE 1947 BRITISH OPEN WINNER, FRED DALY

Long may he live, this grand old golfer! All golfers may be proud of numbering Old Tom [Morris] among their friends. His the native dignity which outweighs all factitious advantages; his the pleasant demeanour, courteous without servility, independent without aggression, which affects favourably to all.

H. EVERARD, *GOLF*, 1891

....

These greens are so fast I have to hold my putter over the ball and hit it with the shadow.

SAM SNEAD, TALKING ABOUT THE GREENS AT AUGUSTA NATIONAL

....

My personal opinion is that more men are good putters from practice than because they have any pronounced superiority, to begin with, over other men.

FRANCIS OUIMET, 1913 UNITED STATES OPEN CHAMPION

If there is one thing I have learned during my years as a professional, it is that the only thing constant about golf is its inconstancy.

JACK NICKLAUS

Always throw clubs ahead of you. That way you don't have to waste energy going back to pick them up.

TOMMY BOLT

The more I practise, the luckier I get.

GARY PLAYER

I can airmail the golf ball, but sometimes I don't put the right address on it.

THE LEGENDARY BIG HITTER, JIM DENT

The difference between Jack and me is that when I got to the top of the mountain in 1974 and 1975, I said, 'Hey, it's time to stop and check out the view.' Whenever Jack reaches the top of a mountain, he starts looking for another.

JOHNNY MILLER, FORMER BRITISH AND US OPEN CHAMPION

I don't think I can ever be another Arnold Palmer. No one could. He can hitch up his pants or yank on a glove and people will start 'oohing' and 'aahing'. When I hitch up mine, nobody notices.

JACK NICKLAUS

I wouldn't bet anyone against Byron Nelson. The only time Nelson left the fairway was to pee in the bushes.

JACKIE BURKE, 1956 US PGA CHAMPION

Jack [Nicklaus] is playing an entirely different game – a game I'm not even familiar with.

BOBBY JONES, AT THE 1965 MASTERS PRESENTATION CEREMONY AT AUGUSTA

That son of a bitch [Bobby] Locke was able to hole a putt over sixty feet of peanut brittle.

LLOYD MANGRUM

He had supernatural strength of mind.

BEN HOGAN, TALKING ABOUT THE GREAT BOBBY JONES

Catching Seve [Ballesteros] is like a Chevy pickup trying to catch a Ferrari

TOM KITE

I'm not sure that the most talented player I ever saw wasn't myself.

JOHNNY MILLER

The only reason I ever played golf in the first place was so I could afford to hunt and fish.

SAM SNEAD

I hate to lose at anything, even at checkers, chess, pool – you name it. I feel if you ease up in any game it breeds a quitting attitude.

TOM WATSON, DISCUSSING THE WILL TO WIN

He's all hands and wrists, like a man dusting furniture.

HENRY LONGHURST, TALKING ABOUT THE INDIVIDUALISTIC GOLF SWING OF THE 1963 US OPEN WINNER, JULIUS BOROS

Nicklaus is a competitor, his thirst for battle, his desire to succeed is equalled only by his instinct to do it all with grace.

BOB WATERS, TODAY'S GOLFER, 1990

If there was a fire on the course while Nick was putting, he'd say: 'What fire? What smoke?'

TONY JACKLIN, ON FALDO'S UNCANNY ABILITY TO
CONCENTRATE

I'm only scared of three things in life – lightning, a side-hill putt and Ben Hogan!

SAM SNEAD

I never thought his short game was very good. Of course, he hit so many greens it didn't make any difference.

TOM WATSON, ABOUT HIS RYDER CUP FOUR-BALL
PARTNER, JACK NICKLAUS, AT WALTON HEATH IN 1981

You couldn't tell whether he was on the right or left of the fairway because his ball was so close to the middle.

DAI REES, ABOUT HENRY COTTON'S ABILITY TO HIT THE
BALL STRAIGHT

When Jack Nicklaus told me I was playing Ballesteros, I took so many pills that I'm glad they don't have drug tests for golfers.

FUZZY ZOELLER, AFTER HIS HALVED SINGLES MATCH
AGAINST SEVE IN THE 1983 RYDER CUP AT THE PGA
NATIONAL

Let me in a few words give you an idea of what Harry is like. In the first place, he differs from me very much, as he is quite nice looking, and is greatly admired by the ladies. Vardon is exceptionally quiet and unassuming, free from the wickedness and vices that often beset young golf professionals. He smokes a briar pipe all the while during a friendly match, is seldom on the aggressive regarding conversation, etc., speaks when he is spoken to, and that very politely. He is passionately fond of golf and association football. The latter is the great winter pastime there [in Britain], and Vardon will go a long distance to witness a game, providing it doesn't clash with his golf appointments.

ALEXANDER H. FINDLAY, FLORIDA GOLF PROFESSIONAL, ASKED TO DESCRIBE THE LEGENDARY HARRY VARDON SHORTLY BEFORE HIS RECORD-BREAKING TOUR OF THE UNITED STATES IN 1900

The groove in his swing was so obvious you could almost see it. I was so impressed that during the last round, when my swing started to leave me, I started imitating his. And it worked, too. Fact is, I almost caught him with his own swing.

WALTER HAGEN, PAIRED WITH HARRY VARDON DURING THE 1913 US OPEN AT BROOKLINE

In practice, McDermott used to hit balls to a newspaper spread on a field, and the story goes that he sometimes got mad if the ball failed to stop on the right paragraph.

CHARLES PRICE, ON THE LEGENDARY AMERICAN PROFESSIONAL, JOHNNY MCDERMOTT, 1962

Playing against him, you begin hoping he'll be on grass rather than in sand. From grass you expect him to pitch the ball close. From a bunker you're afraid he'll hole it out!

JACK NICKLAUS, ON THE SAND PLAY OF RIVAL GARY PLAYER, 1982

Watch the Greyhound! Watch the Greyhound!

ANDREW KIRKALDY, SCOTTISH PROFESSIONAL, WHO WAS
HEARD MUTTERING THIS AFTER HARRY VARDON OVERTOOK
HIM YET AGAIN TO WIN A TOURNAMENT, 1901

Competing ... it's like a drug. It keeps you young. That's what
we are all trying to achieve and playing golf definitely keeps you
young. The average man in the street doesn't realize that. I meet
guys who didn't start playing until they were fifty-something.
They say, 'Gee, if I had started golf in my twenties or thirties I
would be a lot younger and fitter now.'

GARY PLAYER, THE EVER YOUTHFUL WINNER OF GOLF'S
FOUR MAJORS

Eighteen professional majors? Forget it. Nobody will ever
come close, It's the safest record in sport.

GARY PLAYER, ON THE RECORD-BREAKING CAREER OF JACK
NICKLAUS

Seve still has an aura about him, even for me. There are individ-
uals in the world that you are around who you can feel the
energy from. Nelson Mandela was one to me, George Bush was
another and Bill Clinton. People of that ilk have this aura and
you feel it.

GREG NORMAN, ON HIS LONG-TIME RIVAL, SEVE
BALLESTEROS

I wonder why all the golf champions that I have known have always been most agreeable men – that is, the professionals. The amateurs, on the other hand, have not always deserved such high praise. Take James Braid, Sandy Herd, or J. H. Taylor – where will you find better men? I know their companionship does me good, and particularly what I like about them is their keenness. It must be an infernal nuisance for them to play with a bad golfer like myself, yet somehow they give one the impression that they are just as anxious to beat me as if they were playing for the championship.

LORD CASTLEROSS, 1934

I call my sand wedge my half-nelson because I can always strangle the opposition with it.

BYRON NELSON

He is as temperamental as a soprano with a frog in her throat.

CLARENCE B. KELLAND ON THE HARD-LIVING
PROFESSIONAL, TOMMY ARMOUR

His type come and go every year.

CHARLES PRICE, RESPECTED AMERICAN GOLF WRITER,
REPORTING AN EDITOR'S REACTION TO THE IDEA OF
RUNNING A STORY ON RISING STAR ARNOLD PALMER

I'm never going to receive the standing ovations he received throughout the day. I thought a couple of them were for me, then Arnie told me they weren't.

KEN GREEN, ON PARTNERING PALMER IN THE SECOND
ROUND OF THE 1997 MASTERS AT AUGUSTA

He could be the first player to win the Masters who doesn't shave.

Sometimes I think the only way the Spanish people will recognize me is if I win the Grand Slam and then drop dead on the 18th green.

SEVE BALLESTEROS, ON HIS LACK OF RECOGNITION IN HIS HOME COUNTRY, 1979

I didn't beat Merion. I just compromised with her, like a wife, trying not to let her have her way too often.

LEE TREVINO, ON WINNING THE 1971 US OPEN

I have never played golf with anyone, man or woman, amateur or professional who made me feel so utterly outclassed

BOBBY JONES, ON JOYCE WETHERED, 1930

Doesn't take a Rolls Royce long to warm up, does it?

TOMMY AARON, AMERICAN TOURNAMENT PROFESSIONAL, WATCHING GENE LITTLER ON THE PRACTICE TEE, 1970

He swings like an octopus falling from a tree.

GOLF COMMENTATOR, DESCRIBING THE UNUSUAL METHOD OF IRISH RYDER CUP GOLFER EAMONN DARCY

He's a huge inspiration to us. We're lucky to have him on our side. He's great with the crowd and great for the game.

COLIN MONTGOMERIE, ON HIS RYDER CUP TEAM-MATE AT BROOKLINE IN 1999, SERGIO GARCIA

There are several agreeable ways of becoming a millionaire. Winning the football pools is one; claiming the family inheritance is another. Alternatively, you could play golf like Ian Woosnam for a year.

GORDON SIMPSON, *GOLFING GREATS OF GREAT BRITAIN & IRELAND*, 1989

No. When I walk past my trophy cabinet and see those six Order of Merits it gives me a warm glow.

COLIN MONTGOMERIE, ON BEING ASKED WHETHER HE WOULD SWAP HIS EUROPEAN NUMBER-ONE RANKING FOR A MAJOR WIN, 1998

I think it only just to say that, in my opinion, the winning of the above match was due to Tom Morris. Allan [Robertson] was decidedly off his game at the start, and played weakly and badly for a long time – almost justifying the jeers thrown at him, such as 'That wee body in the red jacket canna play gouf', and such like. Tom, on the other hand, played with pluck and determination throughout.

H. THOMAS PETER, DESCRIBING A £400 CHALLENGE MATCH AT NORTH BERWICK IN 1849 BETWEEN THE CHAMPIONS OF ST ANDREWS, TOM MORRIS AND ALLAN ROBERTSON, AND THE DUNN BROTHERS OF MUSSELBURGH, *GOLFING REMINISCENCES OF AN OLD HAND*, 1890.

Championship Golf

Golf, especially championship golf, isn't supposed to be any fun. It was never meant to be fair, and never will make any sense.

CHARLES PRICE

To play well on the final holes of a major championship, you need a certain arrogance. You have to find a trance, some kind of self-hypnosis that's almost a state of grace.

HALE IRWIN

The next morning drove back to Geneva, collected my luggage and arrived back Wednesday night with no time to play a practice round. I shot 79 in the first round, playing with Andrew Murray and a Swiss amateur, and 68 the next day to miss the cut by eight. I thought, 'What is all this about?' I drove back to Geneva for the second time, got on a plane and came home having spent nearly £2,000 in the process. I decided this was not for me. I was going to ask for my amateur status back again but my dad talked me out of it.

COLIN MONTGOMERIE, ON COMPETING IN THE SWISS OPEN EARLY IN HIS CAREER

I won't be content until I score a professional Grand Slam. My ambition is to win the Masters, the US and British Opens and the PGA all in a single year. I think that would be a greater achievement than Bobby Jones's Grand Slam in 1930.

ARNOLD PALMER, IN POSITIVE MOOD AFTER WINNING THE 1960 MASTERS AT AUGUSTA. SADLY, HIS AMBITION WOULD REMAIN UNFULFILLED.

In '78 I had a final round of 64 to win my third green jacket. I came back in 30 that day to win by a shot. Can you imagine it? I also had three lip-outs for birdies. If they had gone in, I would have shot 27 for the last nine holes! If that had happened, I don't think Augusta would have invited me back, do you?

GARY PLAYER, THE ROUND OF MY LIFE, 1998

....

I don't think television work has screwed up my golf. I've pretty much taken care of that on my own.

CURTIS STRANGE, TWICE US OPEN CHAMPION, ON HIS CAREER IN TELEVISION IN THE 1990s

....

Going to Britain is like camping out.

SAM SNEAD, TALKING ABOUT PLAYING IN THE OPEN CHAMPIONSHIP DURING THE POST-WAR YEARS

Nothing compares to the [British] Open. When you are handed that trophy the goose-bumps stand up on the back of your neck looking at the list of previous winners.

SANDY LYLE, BRITISH OPEN CHAMPION, 1985

A horrible species of ping-pong played between the bunkers.

THE SCOTSMAN NEWSPAPER, DESCRIBING THE EFFORTS OF THE AMATEUR, HERMANN TISSIES, AT THE 126-YARD 8TH OR 'POSTAGE STAMP' HOLE IN THE BRITISH OPEN AT TROON IN 1950. AFTER MOVING HIS BALL FROM BUNKER TO BUNKER, HE EVENTUALLY THREE-PUTTED FOR A FIFTEEN – THE SECOND HIGHEST SCORE IN THE HISTORY OF THE EVENT.

I don't think people appreciate how hard we work, and mentally how hard it is to win a Major.

NICK FALDO

It will take a plodder to win this championship. A player who plods on and on, a player to whom nothing much happens.

COLIN MONTGOMERIE PREDICTING THE OUTCOME OF THE 1993 UNITED STATES OPEN AT BALTUSROL. IT WAS EVENTUALLY WON BY LEE JANZEN.

Playing the US Open is like tippy-toeing through hell.

JERRY MCGEE

I've been getting pumped up for the [US] Open and similar championships for 42 years. I suppose when the day comes that I'm not excited and I don't have some rumblings in my stomach, I won't play ... but somewhere in my make-up and thinking there might be a chance I could win again.

ARNOLD PALMER, WHOSE LAST MAJOR WIN CAME IN THE US MASTERS IN 1964

Hit it here, fat boy.

PLACARD HELD UP BY FANS OF ARNOLD PALMER IN THE
EARLY DAYS OF JACK NICKLAUS'S CAREER

You'd think I'd never done anything else but hit that shot
(which won the US Masters in 1935). In the Orient for a while
I became known as Mr Double Eagle, which non-golfers probably took to mean that I was an Indian chief.

GENE SARAZEN

I would have shot the cat if it sang out of tune as badly as they
did.

NICK FALDO, AFTER SPECTATORS AT ROYAL BIRKDALE SANG
'HAPPY BIRTHDAY' TO HIM ON THE SATURDAY OF THE 1998
OPEN

....

*The professional golf watcher never catches the action. I could write a volume
on Great Moments in Golf I Have Missed.*

PETER DOBEREINER

....

I'm definitely not a pioneer. That's for people like Jackie
Robinson and Lee Elder. I'm just a product of their hard work.

TIGER WOODS, ON THE GROUND-BREAKING WORK OF BLACK
PROFESSIONALS

Tournament organizers and sponsors should insist upon playing golf on courses which do not use artificial green-keeping
methods. I disagree totally with the policy of measuring each

hole, publishing yardage charts and offering information about exact pin positions. That makes it little more than a form of target golf. The game should be played with the eye only.

FRED DALY, IRISH-BORN RYDER CUP PLAYER, ON THE GROWING RELIANCE OF TOURNAMENT PLAYERS ON YARDAGE CHARTS

You can play a damned good shot there and find the ball in a damned bad place.

GEORGE DUNCAN, BRITISH OPEN WINNER IN 1920, ON ST ANDREWS

....

If you can imagine a hole half-way down the bonnet of a Volkswagen Beetle, and then you have to putt it from the roof.

NICK FALDO, DESCRIBING THE GREENS AT ROYAL MELBOURNE GOLF CLUB IN 1990

....

In Britain, you skip the ball, hop it, bump it, run it, hit on top of it and then hope for the right bounce.

DOUG SANDERS, ON PLAYING LINKS GOLF

We're not trying to humiliate the greatest players in the world. We're trying to identify them.

FRANK TATUM, FORMER USGA PRESIDENT, ON THE INCREASINGLY TOUGH STANDARD OF THOSE COURSES CHOSEN FOR THE US OPEN

I have never felt so lonely as on a golf course in the midst of a championship with thousands of people around, especially when things began to go wrong and the crowds started wandering away.

Bobby Jones

One other important thing about this victory, it proved that my British Open victory was no fluke. It's always been my contention that the winners of major tournaments are the true champions, although at times some luck may play a part in the victory. Naturally, after I won the British Open, I entertained some suspicious thoughts about luck, but when I won the US Open, this was all dissolved.

Tony Jacklin, on winning the 1970 US Open at Hazeltine

I can't see why I broke so badly. Why, I am sure I could go out now and do better by kicking the ball around with my boot.

Harry Vardon, on his score of 78 in the final round of the US Open in 1920

To me, the [British] Open is the tournament I would come to if I had to leave a month before and swim over.

Lee Trevino

I hit a hook that went so far out of bounds I almost killed a horse in some stables a cab ride from the first fairway. I was so nervous I didn't have the strength to push the tee in the ground.

Mike Souchak on making his debut in the Los Angeles Open

Ben wants to know the place so well that he could give a biologist a thorough life history of the four rabbits who hole up off the 14th fairway.

JIMMY DEMARET, ON HOGAN'S METICULOUS APPROACH TO TOURNAMENT GOLF

If he had needed a 64 on the last round, you were quite certain he could have played a 64. Hogan gave the distinct impression he was capable of getting whatever score was needed to win.

BERNARD DARWIN, BRITISH GOLF WRITER, AFTER BEN HOGAN SHOT A CLOSING 68 TO WIN THE 1953 BRITISH OPEN AT CARNOUSTIE

The first time I played here, back in 1959, I'll never forget it. People looked at me as if I had a tail.

CHARLIE SIFFORD, ON BEING A BLACK GOLF PROFESSIONAL AT THE 1974 US OPEN AT WINGED FOOT

It was just a typical British day.

TOM WATSON, ON HIS BRILLIANT 69 IN TORRENTIAL RAIN AND 30MPH WINDS ON HIS WAY TO WINNING THE 1979 MEMORIAL TOURNAMENT AT MUIRFIELD VILLAGE. MOST OF HIS RIVALS STRUGGLED TO BREAK 80.

I only remember the bad ones.

BEN HOGAN, WHEN ASKED TO RECALL HIS GREATEST EVER SHOT

I don't want to take anything away from Jack. He played fantastic golf. But I think for me not to win was almost a miracle under the circumstances. Eight out of ten times I would have won. It has to be destiny.

SEVE BALLESTEROS, IN REFLECTIVE MOOD AFTER SURRENDERING A TWO-STROKE LEAD TO JACK NICKLAUS IN THE FINAL STAGES OF THE 1986 US MASTERS AT AUGUSTA

I wouldn't advise any professional golfer to marry before the age of thirty. Marriage means a division of interests, and golf, particularly tournament golf, demands all your time.

HENRY COTTON, THREE TIMES WINNER OF THE BRITISH OPEN

I never felt I could be a complete professional without having won the British Open. It was something you had to do to complete your career.

ARNOLD PALMER, TWICE WINNER OF THE BRITISH OPEN

Water creates a neurosis in golfers. The very thought of this harmless fluid robs them of their normal powers of rational thought, turns their legs to jelly, and produces a palsy of the upper limbs.

PETER DOBEREINER, BRITISH GOLF WRITER

Individually, they are pretty nice folks. But get them together and they are about as miserable a bunch of people as you could ever have the misfortune to run into in a supposedly civilised world.

TOMMY BOLT, AMERICAN RYDER CUP PLAYER, ON THE BRITISH GOLFING PUBLIC

There isn't a hole out there that can't be birdied if you just think. But there isn't one that can't be double-bogeyed if you stop thinking.

BOBBY JONES, ON AUGUSTA NATIONAL GOLF CLUB, HOME OF THE MASTERS

The professional, as we are now chiefly acquainted with him, is a feckless, reckless creature. In the golfing season in Scotland he makes his money all the day, and spends it all the night. His sole loves are golf and whisky.

HORACE HUTCHINSON, BRITISH GOLF WRITER, ON THE STANDARD OF SCOTTISH GOLF PROFESSIONALS AROUND THE TURN OF THE CENTURY

We always considered it quite a feat to get down our six-to-eight footers, but now if a fellow misses from forty feet he grimaces and agonizes like a cowboy struck in the heart by an Indian's arrow.

BEN HOGAN

There's an old saying on tour: set fire to the trees and cover the greens with broken glass, put the pros out there in gasoline-soaked pants and barefooted, and someone will break par.

Tommy Bolt, on the standard of tournament professionals in the 1960s

Spectators sometimes view games of golf, but as a rule they stand far off, for the nature of the implements employed is such that a ball may be driven in a very contrary direction to that which the player wishes, and therefore may fall among the spectators and cause some temporary discomfort. Moreover it would require considerable activity upon the part of the spectators to watch the play in golf, for they would have to run around and see how every hole was gained, from one end of the game to the other. There may be as many as thirty spectators at one game, but seldom more, and a good game is frequently played without any at all.

The Philadelphia Times, offering some guidelines for watching golf in 1889. By way of comparison, the 1999 Ryder Cup in Boston was limited to 25,000 spectators per day!

The boy is a genius. If he ever learns to play he will be unbeatable.

John Jacobs, on Seve Ballesteros's performance in the 1976 British Open at Royal Birkdale

I am still young. When I am older there will be time to be careful.

Seve Ballesteros, aged just 19, shortly after his second-place finish in the 1976 British Open

Moderation is essential in all things, Madam, but never in my life have I failed to beat a teetotaller.

HARRY VARDON, SIX TIMES BRITISH OPEN CHAMPION, WHEN ASKED TO JOIN THE TEMPERANCE MOVEMENT, 1915

You don't have to talk, Tony, just listen.

LEE TREVINO REPLYING TO JACKLIN'S REQUEST FOR NO TALKING DURING THE FINAL ROUND OF THE 1972 BRITISH OPEN AT MUIRFIELD. THE AMERICAN EVENTUALLY EDGED OUT JACKLIN INTO THIRD PLACE TO RECORD HIS SECOND CONSECUTIVE WIN IN THE EVENT.

I wonder who will come second?

WALTER HAGEN'S USUAL OPENING REMARK AT A MAJOR CHAMPIONSHIP

At times, the past few years have just flown by. Other times, they have dragged. Now I look back and think, 'Well, if someone had said when I was 16 that you can have the Masters and the Open, I would have snapped their hand off.'

SANDY LYLE, *THE ROUND OF MY LIFE*, 1998

On the golf course you can't feel sorry for anybody. You have to try to win the golf tournament. You're not beating the guy you're playing against, you're beating the course. And that's probably life. I've got to live with it, and they've got to live with it.

ERNIE ELS, SOUTH AFRICAN PROFESSIONAL AND US OPEN WINNER

If long hitting is the thing that causes the spectators to whistle through their teeth in wonderment, why not play tournaments up and down an expansive stadium?

ROBERT HARRIS, *SIXTY YEARS OF GOLF*, 1953

Nowadays the competition for the Majors is so strong, with maybe thirty or forty players able to win. Thirty years ago only about ten could win. It's the same with regular Tour events. I think you have to be happy with winning one tournament a year, let alone a Major.

FRED COUPLES, ON THE RISING STANDARD OF TOURNAMENT GOLF, 1996

You can't always be playing well when it counts. You'll never win golf tournaments until you learn to score well when you're playing badly.

JIM BARNES, 1925 BRITISH OPEN WINNER

I can't describe how I feel. It's the greatest thing in the world to win a professional golf tournament – especially if you're a professional golfer.

DAVE EICHELBURGER, AMERICAN PROFESSIONAL AND WINNER OF THE 1977 MILWAUKEE OPEN

I paid £1000 for this car. That was a lot of money back in the Fifties. So my last words to my wife at London airport were, 'If I don't win the Open, I'll have to sell this damn car.' Well, I wasn't going to let that happen, was I?

MAX FAULKNER, ON HIS INCENTIVE FOR WINNING THE 1951 BRITISH OPEN AT ROYAL PORTRUSH

I'm known as a hot-dog pro. That's when someone in the gallery looks at his pairing sheet and says, 'Here comes Joe Baloney, Sam Sausage, and Chi Chi Rodriguez – let's go get a hot dog.'

CHI CHI RODRIGUEZ, AT THE 1964 US PGA
CHAMPIONSHIP

I think anytime you are in the hunt for a Major championship, you learn something about yourself.

TOM LEHMAN, SHORTLY AFTER WINNING THE 1996
BRITISH OPEN AT ROYAL LYTHAM AND ST ANNES

Ask any top professional playing today about what it means to win their first Major. The first one is always tough, perhaps the toughest. The second one is also hard, but the third is definitely not as tough as the other two. It's like the hurdle is twenty feet high. Then once you have won your first major it's like six inches and you feel you can just hop over the thing. That's maybe why experienced players, Major winners for example, find they have an advantage coming down the stretch of any tournament. They know what it takes to win and that is something you cannot buy.

NICK PRICE, THE ROUND OF MY LIFE, 1998

The number one thought [at the US Open] is to keep the ball in the fairway. It's like a game of chess. You have to put the ball in play first – so that man doesn't get captured.

TOM WATSON, WINNER OF THE 1982 US OPEN AT PEBBLE
BEACH

I sure am glad we don't have to play in the shade then.

WALTER HAGEN, ON BEING INFORMED THAT THE
EXHIBITION MATCH HE HAD PLAYED IN TOOK PLACE IN 100-
DEGREE HEAT

I think this is the only tournament I've ever gone into that I'm hoping I can finish second. That would be the neat part.

JACK NICKLAUS, ROOTING FOR HIS SON GARY TO WIN THE
US OPEN IN 1996

Everybody in my family is talented. My father, my mother, my brother, my sister Mary. She shot 'J. R.' [Ewing]. Gosh, I had to win the Amateur.

NATHANIEL CROSBY, SON OF CROONER BING, AFTER
WINNING THE US AMATEUR CHAMPIONSHIP IN 1981

Everybody has two swings: the one he uses during the last three holes of a tournament and the one he uses the rest of the time.

TONEY PENNA, AMERICAN PROFESSIONAL TURNED CLUB
DESIGNER

If I miss one day's practice I know it; if I miss two days the spectators know it, and if I miss three days the world knows it.

BEN HOGAN

I was like a swan – gliding on top with my legs paddling madly underneath.

LEE WESTWOOD, ON THE PRESSURE HE FELT WHEN
LEADING THE 1998 FREEPORT McDERMOTT CLASSIC ON
THE FINAL DAY

If you can bring the ship home with cargo and crew intact through the hurricane of the last day, that's an achievement. Right?

MAC O'GRADY, THE EMINENTLY QUOTABLE GOLF PRO
TURNED GOLF COACH, DISCUSSING A BAD ROUND IN 1987

Out there you are either bleeding, haemorrhaging, or painting Mona Lisas.

MAC O'GRADY DURING THE US OPEN, 1987

You know what I did here one year? I was so nervous I drank a fifth of rum before I played. I shot the happiest 83 of my life.

CHI CHI RODRIGUEZ

Out here, you've got to realize that if you take an eight on a hole, 90 per cent of the other pros don't care and the other ten per cent wish it had been a nine.

MASON RUDOLPH, AT THE 1969 TUCSON OPEN

Golf championships are a good deal like omelettes. You cannot have an omelette without breaking eggs, and you cannot have a golf championship without wrecking hopes.

O. B. KEELER, AMERICAN GOLF WRITER

Any player can win a US Open, but it takes a hell of a player to win two.

WALTER HAGEN, WINNER OF TWO US OPEN TITLES

Nobody wins the [US] Open. It wins you.

DR CARY MIDDLECOFF

All of a sudden I'm an expert on everything. Interviewers want your opinion of golf, foreign policy and even the price of peanuts.

HUBERT GREEN, SHORTLY AFTER WINNING THE 1977 US OPEN AT SOUTHERN HILLS

Hey, hurry up, Gene, I've got a date tonight.

WALTER HAGEN TO GENE SARAZEN, MOMENTS BEFORE HE HOLED HIS SECOND SHOT ON THE PAR-FIVE 15TH AT AUGUSTA ON HIS WAY TO WINNING THE 1935 MASTERS

The worst thing that can happen is for somebody to click a camera in a player's backswing. The media photographers who are out here go to great pains not to violate that rule. But the fans carrying these little box cameras have become a real problem. I've told some people they aren't supposed to have cameras. Some don't know. Some just don't care.

DAVIS LOVE III, ON AMATEUR PHOTOGRAPHERS AT GOLF TOURNAMENTS

How in the world did they ever get that? I've never been to New York in my life.

SAM SNEAD, ON BEING SHOWN A PICTURE OF HIMSELF IN THE NEW YORK PAPERS AFTER WINNING THE 1937 OAKLAND OPEN

I have never been more scared in my life on a golf course than I was at Brookline. It was frightening to hear people shouting 'Kill, kill' and 'Bring out the body bags'.

KEN SCHOFIELD, EUROPEAN TOUR EXECUTIVE DIRECTOR, ON THE CROWD PROBLEMS AT THE 1999 RYDER CUP AT BROOKLINE

The biggest thing is to have the mind-set and the belief you can win every tournament going in. A lot of guys don't have that; Nicklaus had it. He felt he was going to beat everybody.

TIGER WOODS

I think a little competition is a good thing as it makes one study one's game and makes one more keen to play well, but it is that continual pot-hunting which is much in fashion now-a-days, that tends to make golf too much of a business and does away, to my mind, with half the fun of the game.

S. MURE FERGUSSON, TOP BRITISH AMATEUR, 1914

My enthusiasm for the game has dwindled in that I've found something more interesting than golf – a wife.

BRUCE LEITZKE, AMERICAN RYDER CUP GOLFER, ON HIS DWINDLING INTEREST IN TOURNAMENT GOLF IN THE EARLY 1980s

Why would I want to be out there with all those young guns? No sense playing the flat bellies when I can play the round bellies.

LEE TREVINO, LOOKING FORWARD TO PLAYING ON THE SENIORS TOUR, 1989

If you don't enjoy pressure, you're in the wrong place.

JUSTIN LEONARD, TALKING ABOUT MODERN-DAY
TOURNAMENT GOLF

The flags on this golf course should be at half-mast.

MAX FAULKNER, 1951 BRITISH OPEN WINNER, TALKING
ABOUT A PARTICULARLY BAD ROUND

The things that look easiest in golf are usually the hardest —
take putting, for example.

ERIC BROWN, FORMER BRITISH RYDER CUP CAPTAIN

I remember there was a guy from Dunlop who was giving out
free balls on the practice ground. I didn't speak English so I say
to my brother Manuel, 'You know this is a very difficult course
and I need plenty golf balls.' So he introduced me to this man
and tells him I am a very good golfer, so he will give me some
to play with during the week. So he takes out a dozen and gives
me a box of three balls. I say to Manuel, 'This is good. That will
be enough for six holes; what about the rest of the tournament?'
So he ask the man again and he says to me real serious, 'If you
make the cut on Saturday I will give three more, OK?' That
shows how much things have changed on tour. These days I get
six dozen per week.

SEVE BALLESTEROS, ON THE CHANGING FACE OF
TOURNAMENT GOLF IN THE 1990s

....

*I just felt so proud to win the Open Championship. This is the Olympics of
golf, the oldest and the biggest of the Majors. But even then it took a while to*

sink in. The weeks after Lytham were so busy, my schedule was so hectic, that I didn't have much time to think about it. The Old Claret Jug was sitting on my mantelpiece back home in Arizona but it was so revered by all the family that I hardly touched it, not even to polish it. I think it really came home to me a short time later when some teenage kids came up to my door 'Trick or Treating' during Halloween. They knew who I was and asked could they see the trophy. They just huddled around it, reading off the famous names that were on it — Nicklaus, Palmer ... They were really excited and that made me feel good about winning it. Then I really felt like an Open champion.

TOM LEHMAN, *THE ROUND OF MY LIFE*, 1998

....

I sometimes look at guys who have won Majors and they seem different somehow. Justin has gotten to be a good friend of mine, but I look at him and I don't see Justin Leonard anymore, I see Justin Leonard, [British] Open Champion, and that's a big difference.

DAVIS LOVE III, SHORTLY BEFORE WINNING THE 1997 US PGA CHAMPIONSHIP AT WINGED FOOT

No doubt the public knows less about the inside intricacies of first-class golf than of any other sport. It seems to be their particular delight to watch a famous golfer miss a shot and then hold him up to ridicule.

TOMMY ARMOUR

I have four wives.

A COMPETITOR FROM NEW GUINEA FILLING IN THE SECTION ON A TOURNAMENT ENTRANCE FORM WHICH ASKED, 'ANY UNUSUAL ACHIEVEMENTS?'

Everything has been pretty normal, no overdosing on volcanic dust. I kept it pretty simple.

JESPER PARNEVIK, DESCRIBING HIS RUN-UP TO THE 1998 US OPEN

It's incredible the way the USGA can limit scoring. There was not one pin position that was a gift.

COLIN MONTGOMERIE, ON THE CONTROVERSIAL PIN PLACEMENTS DURING THE SECOND ROUND OF THE 1998 US OPEN

If you hit the fairways you have a chance to score. If you don't, you're DOA [dead on arrival].

OLIN BROWNE, AFTER HIS THREE-OVER-PAR OPENING ROUND IN THE 1998 US OPEN

I come to the US Open expecting nothing to be fair. So it's a test of wills to find out who overcomes adversity the best and who has the most patience.

LEE JANZEN ON THE EVE OF THE 1998 US OPEN

People get aggressive and tend to crowd in and it can get pretty ugly out there. Adults are even knocking over kids to get an autograph.

TIGER WOODS, ON THE TRIALS OF BEING A SUPERSTAR

There was nothing wrong with the Ryder Cup except you lost.

COLIN MONTGOMERIE'S RETORT TO A NOISY SPECTATOR AT THE 1998 US OPEN

It makes you feel good, but you don't feel good if you're not playing well enough to warrant it. I hate walking up the 18th shooting 165 and saying, 'Gee, hi everybody.' I don't want to embarrass myself.

JACK NICKLAUS, ON RECEIVING STANDING OVATIONS WHEREVER HE PLAYS

Now on the pot, Johnny Tee.

ANNOUNCER ON THE FIRST HOLE OF THE 1963 LOS ANGELES OPEN, INTRODUCING THE PROFESSIONAL, JOHNNY POTT

My putter had a heart attack the last nine holes and just died on me.

LANNY WADKINS, ON THE REASON FOR HIS FINAL-ROUND COLLAPSE IN THE BYRON NELSON CLASSIC, 1973

If you're not prepared, somewhere in the quiz there are going to be some questions you can't answer.

CHARLES COODY, ON THE NEED FOR PRACTICE BEFORE, DURING AND AFTER A GOLF TOURNAMENT

The Masters is more like a vast Edwardian garden party than a golf tournament.

ALISTAIR COOKE

You always have butterflies in your stomach, but these butter-flies are playing hockey.

MIKE REID, THIRD-ROUND LEADER IN THE US PGA CHAMPIONSHIP, 1989

Equipped for Golf

Perhaps the most important thing I can tell you about equipment is to experiment and keep an open mind.

GARY PLAYER

We speak of eyeball-to-eyeball encounters between men great and small. Even more searching and revealing of character is the eyeball-to-golf ball confrontation, whereby our most secret natures are mercilessly tested by a small, round, whitish object with no mind or will but with a very definite life of its own, and with whims perverse and beatific.

JOHN STUART MARTIN, AUTHOR OF *THE CURIOUS HISTORY OF THE GOLF BALL – MAN'S MOST FASCINATING SPHERE*

....

[The golf ball] is white, dimpled like a bishop's knees, and is the size of small mandarin oranges or those huge pills which vets blow down the throats of constipated cart-horses.

FRANK MUIR, ENGLISH AUTHOR AND WIT

....

If I'd played the big ball I'd have been all over the place.

WALTER DANECKI'S DESCRIPTION OF HIS TWO OPEN
CHAMPIONSHIP QUALIFYING ROUNDS OF 108 AND 113 AT
HILLSIDE IN 1965. ENTERING THE EVENT AS A
PROFESSIONAL, HE WAS, IN FACT, A MAIL SORTER WHOSE
GOLF EXPERIENCE WAS LIMITED TO A FEW ROUNDS ON HIS
LOCAL PUBLIC COURSE IN MILWAUKIE. HE FAILED TO
QUALIFY FOR THE OPEN CHAMPIONSHIP BY 75 STROKES,
FORCING THE R&A TO DRASTICALLY BEEF UP THEIR
QUALIFYING PROCEDURE.

The ball is undoubtedly the controlling factor in the game.
Its evolution and development to the final state in which it
is now used is a gradual process of invention and improvement until it has reached a position where it dominates golf
too much and threatens to destroy the character of the
game as a sport. The power of the ball unbalances the traditional method of play and makes the game a labour of
long-distance walking.

ROBERT HARRIS, *SIXTY YEARS OF GOLF*, 1953

The making of first-class feather balls was almost a science. For
the benefit of the uninitiated, I shall endeavour to explain the
operation. The leather was of untanned bull's hide. Two round
pieces for the ends, and a stripe for the middle were cut to suit
the weight wanted. These were properly shaped, after being suf-
ficiently softened and firmly sewed together – a small hole being
of course left, through which the feathers might be afterwards

inserted. But, before stuffing, it was through this little hole that the leather itself bad to be turned outside in, so that the seams should be inside – an operation not without difficulty.

> H. THOMAS PETER, *GOLFING REMINISCENCES BY AN OLD HAND*, 1890

The trade [of feather ball making] is commonly fatal to the artists, for the balls are made by stuffing a great quantity of feathers into a leather case, by help of an iron, with a wooden handle, pressed against the breast, which seldom fails to bring on consumption.

> THOMAS PENNANT, ON THE HAZARDS INVOLVED IN MAKING GOLF BALLS IN THE MID-EIGHTEENTH CENTURY, *PENNANT'S TOUR OF SCOTLAND*, 1790

A professional will tell you the amount of flex you need in the shaft of your club. The more the flex, the more strength you will need to break the thing over your knees.

> STEPHEN BAKER, AMERICAN WRITER

What are you gonna do, build a bonfire?

> GEORGE LOW, AMERICAN CLUB PROFESSIONAL, WATCHING A MEMBER DIPPING HIS HAND INTO A BOX OF FREE WOODEN TEES

Honey, why don't you quit kidding yourself? It just can't be entirely the clubs. Your trouble is you!

> LOUISE NELSON, OFFERING SOME ADVICE TO HUSBAND BYRON IN 1936

I am afraid players pay too much attention to appearance and too little to balance. A club may have a most finished appearance, but nevertheless be a terrible sinner in the outward guise of a complete saint.

HAROLD HILTON, *THE ROYAL & ANCIENT GAME OF GOLF*, 1912

Whereas the clubs used in golf have now been partially standardised, the putter has retained its individuality. It may be made of wood, iron, brass, or aluminium; there are those with wry necks, goose necks, bottle necks, necks like corkscrews; straight faced, long faced, curved faced; fitted with long handles, short handles, square grips, oval grips, round grips – and just grips. In fact their number is legion.

H. MACNEILE DIXON, *GOLF AND HOW*, 1944

A ball on the match is a good thing. It is a tangible result of victory, a punishment to the loser, a reward to the winner.

LETTER TO *GOLFER MAGAZINE* FROM 'A CONCERNED READER', 1890

About 1906, the Goodyear people, who had helped Doctor Haskell in perfecting the original rubber-cored ball, placed on the market a ball called the Pneumatic. This ball had a rubber cover or shell into which air was compressed. It caught the fancy of the golfers for a time, but the Pneumatic had to be hit powerfully in order to get it along. The younger element had fair success with it, because they could hit harder and therefore got the better results. It lacked the resiliency of the rubber-cored balls, and although it was fairly durable in so far as cutting the cover was concerned, it had other faults which were distressing. Many times it was knocked out of shape, and when this did not occur it exploded either in flight or in the caddie bags. Golfers had many interesting experiences with the Pneumatic.

FRANCIS OUIMET, 1913 US OPEN CHAMPION

....

Golf: a game in which a ball one and a half inches in diameter is placed on a ball eight thousand miles in diameter. The object is to hit the small ball but not the larger.

JOHN CUNNINGHAM, AMERICAN AUTHOR

....

Of the clubs there are six sorts used by proficients; viz. The common club, when the ball lies on the ground; the scraper and half-scraper, when in long grass; the spoon when in a hollow; the heavy iron club, when it lies deep among the stones or mud; and the light iron club, when on the surface of shingle or sandy ground. All these clubs are tapered at the part that strikes the ball; they are also faced with horn, and loaded with lead.

HOYLES' GAMES, IMPROVED NEW EDITION, 1816

There are eleven implements of the game, the most important of which is the ball. This is made of gutta-percha and is painted white. It weighs about two ounces and is just small enough to fit comfortably into the holes dug in the ground. Still it should not be so large that it cannot be taken out with ease. The other ten implements are the tools of the players. Their names are as follows: the playing club, long spoon, mud spoon, short spoon, baffing spoon, driving putter, putter, sand iron, club and track iron. Each of these is about four feet long, the entire length of which in general consists of a wooden handle. The head is spliced on, and may be either metal or wood. The handle, as a rule, is made of hickory covered with leather.

THE PHILADELPHIA TIMES, DESCRIBING WHAT WAS IN A
TYPICAL GOLFER'S BAG, 1889

Knickers (plus-fours) are good for my golf game. They're cooler in hot weather because the air circulates in them and they're warmer in cold weather because they trap the body heat.

PAYNE STEWART, FORMER US OPEN CHAMPION,
DESCRIBING HIS UNUSUAL GOLFING ATTIRE

I wonder what Tommy Morris would have had to say to all this number 6-iron, number 12-iron, number 28-iron stuff. He probably wouldn't have said anything, just made one of those strange Scottish noises at the back of his throat like someone gargling.

P. G. WODEHOUSE

On top of my interest in the game itself, I took a tremendous interest in the clubs and balls, particularly the latter. I had seen many changes in the golf ball, and I believe the great development in the game of golf is directly attributable to the wonderful strides made by the manufacturers in perfecting the ball and making the game a more pleasant one to play.

FRANCIS OUIMET, 1913 US OPEN CHAMPION

There is a serious thought that the game is now in process of decline as a result of over-mechanization; art and skill are being replaced by lust for distance of hit.

ROBERT HARRIS, *SIXTY YEARS OF GOLF*, 1953

A niblick is an iron-headed club, deep in the face; and of this club there are two main varieties. The one with a thin blade and knife-like sole and the other more heavily built, weighing anything up to two stone, only to be wielded by the golfing giants, known as the 'Blaster' – in fact, the rapier and the battle-axe of the golfing world. Both weapons I find have one thing in common: they cut the cover off any ball.

H. MACNEILE DIXON, *GOLF AND HOW*, 1944

Why am I using a new putter? Because the last one didn't float too well.

CRAIG 'THE WALRUS' STADLER, THE POPULAR AMERICAN PROFESSIONAL

The divorce is from my old putter. I think it's final – at least we're due for a long separation. I've suffered with that old putter for two years now. It got so rude I couldn't stand it.

SHELLY HAMLIN, FORMER US LPGA TOUR PROFESSIONAL

The less said about the putter the better. Here is an instrument of torture, designed by Tantalus and forged in the devil's own smithy.

TONY LEMA, 1964 BRITISH OPEN CHAMPION

Hickory golf was a game of manipulation and inspiration; steel golf is a game of precision and calculation.

PETER DOBEREINER, NOTED BRITISH GOLF WRITER 1973

Polyclubia-Inanis – this is a very peculiar disease, being by no manner of means confined to beginners; in fact, it often reaches an acute form of mania in otherwise very fine players. It consists of an unconquerable desire to be possessed of any certain club with which either the rightful owner in the patient's presence, or the patient himself when trying it, has made a fine shot. He generally endeavours to acquire the club, and I am bound to say is willing to pay a price quite incommensurate with its real value. Consequently clubs accumulate to an almost alarming degree.

TIMOTHY WARD, *SOME DISEASES OF GOLF*, 1896

In tennis you seldom have a chance, once things get going, to get shaky. You're too busy running around like a racehorse. Golf – hell, it makes me nervous just to talk about it. That little white ball just sits there. A man can beat himself before he ever swings at it.

THE MULTI-TALENTED ELLSWORTH VINES, AN AMERICAN
TENNIS PROFESSIONAL WHO LATER BECAME A GOLF PRO

The one-iron is almost unplayable. You keep it in your bag the way you keep a Dostoevsky novel in your bookcase – with the vague notion that you will try it some day. In the meantime, it impresses your friends.

TOM SCOTT, BRITISH GOLF WRITER

Hard by, in the fields called the Links, the citizens of Edinburgh divert themselves at a game called Golf, in which they use a curious kind of bats tipped with horn, and small elastic balls of leather, stuffed with feathers, rather less than tennis balls, but of a much harder consistence. These they strike with such force and dexterity from one hole to another, that they will fly to an incredible distance. Of this diversion the Scots are so fond, that, when the weather will permit, you may see a multitude of all ranks, from the senator of justice to the lowest tradesman, mingled together, in their shirts, and following the balls with the utmost eagerness.

TOBIAS SMOLLETT, *THE EXPEDITION OF HUMPHRY CLINKER*, 1771

The two-iron had already earned thousands of pounds for charity, although it wasn't always the club that went on show. When I won the Kenya Open in 1992, a nun approached me and asked if she could auction the two-iron for a good cause. I told her it wasn't the original and she said, 'Who'll know the difference?'

CHRISTY O' CONNOR, ON THE TWO-IRON THAT HELPED HIM AND THE EUROPEANS RETAIN THE RYDER CUP AT THE BELFRY IN 1989

If you do that once more I shall break your bloody neck!

BRITISH GOLF WRITER PAT WARD-THOMAS, AFTER TOPPING THREE SUCCESSIVE FAIRWAY WOOD SHOTS IN LATER LIFE. A FORMER PRISONER-OF-WAR IN GERMANY, HE IS BEST KNOWN FOR HAVING DESIGNED AND BUILT A SHORT PAR-THREE COURSE INSIDE THE CAMP

The strangest man I ever knew on the links was a regular opponent, of middle age and middle handicap. At once let it
be remembered that he was a man of kindliest character, which
he hid beneath fierce austerity of look and a power of invective
that were matchless in their time. His clubs seemed for ever to
be on the verge of total collapse; there was a driver from which
string and plaster flapped protestingly; a mongrel mid-iron,
withered and rusty, with which he played what he was pleased
to call his 'push-shot'; a putter that was wry-necked and,
though, I suppose, within the law, yet against equity and nature.

R. C. ROBERTSON-GLASGOW

The trouble that most of us find with the modern matched sets
of clubs is that they don't really seem to know any more about
the game than the old ones did!

ROBERT BROWNING, *A HISTORY OF GOLF*, 1955

I wish I could say that my Ti-2 driver was nuclear, but unfortunately Tiger still hit it 80 yards by me.

MARK O'MEARA, ON THE DIFFERENCE IN DRIVING
DISTANCE BETWEEN HIM AND TIGER WOODS

They want to make sure the windows are closed, otherwise
they'll find my Titleist Balata in their Caesar Salad.

WAYNE RILEY, EUROPEAN TOUR PROFESSIONAL,
CONCERNED THAT THE CORPORATE ENCLOSURE AT THE
1998 AUSTRALIAN OPEN WAS ONLY SIX FEET FROM THE
BACK EDGE OF THE 18TH GREEN

It's good sportsmanship not to pick up lost golf balls while they are still rolling.

MARK TWAIN

If I had my way, I'd never let the sand be raked. Instead, I'd run a herd of elephants through them every morning.

CHARLES BLAIR MACDONALD, AMERICAN GOLF COURSE ARCHITECT, ON THE INTRODUCTION OF THE SAND RAKE, 1920s

---

A Birmingham gentleman has invented steel shafts for golf clubs. So far the invention has proved highly successful and the shafts will be placed upon the market at a very early date.

LE GOLF, A FRENCH GOLF MAGAZINE, DESCRIBING IN SIMPLE TERMS THE GREATEST LEAP FORWARD IN GOLF EQUIPMENT IN FIVE CENTURIES, 1914

Clothes may not make the man, but they certainly make the golfer, and no well-established player would come to the links improperly dressed, any more than he would sit down at a public dinner without having assumed the black coat of formality.

H. MACNEILE DIXON, GOLF AND HOW, 1944

Do not be tempted to invest in a sample of each golfing invention as soon as it makes its appearance. If you do, you will only complicate and spoil your game – and encumber your locker with much useless rubbish.

HARRY VARDON

God and Golf

The determining bulk of Scotch people had heard of golf ever since they had heard of God and often considered the two as of equal importance.

G. K. CHESTERTON

Golf: the second best pastime that any sinner on this earth can have.

R. H. LYTTELTON

There are now more golf clubs in the world than Gideon Bibles, more golf balls than missionaries and, if every golfer in the world, male and or female, were laid end to end, I for one would leave them there.

MICHAEL PARKINSON, FORMER FOUNDER MEMBER OF THE ANTI-GOLF SOCIETY

If profanity had an influence on the flight of the ball, the game would be played far better than it is.

HORACE HUTCHINSON

If God were a teenager and descended to give us the Word, He'd probably look like Hal Sutton.

NATHANIAL CROSBY, SON OF BING AND FORMER US AMATEUR CHAMPION

I wouldn't care if I got beat by twenty shots. I'd still like to see how God does it.

ED FIORI, US TOUR PROFESSIONAL, ON BEING PAIRED WITH NICKLAUS

I call my putter 'Sweet Charity' because it covers such a multitude of sins from tee to green.

GARDNER DICKINSON

I'll tell you why putts go in. Because the old National Open Champion in the sky puts 'em in.

BOB ROSBURGH

And don't send your Son down. This is a man's job.

BERNARD DARWIN, NOTED BRITISH GOLF WRITER, REVIEWING A POOR LIE IN A BUNKER

The only place over there that's holier than St Andrews is Westminster Abbey.

SAM SNEAD, *THE EDUCATION OF A GOLFER*, 1962

My God, it looks like a wax museum!

GEORGE LOW, FORMER US TOURING PRO, AT HIS FIRST SENIORS EVENT, 1980

Actually, the Lord answers my prayers everywhere except on the golf course.

BILLY GRAHAM, WORLD-FAMOUS EVANGELIST

He enjoys that perfect peace, that peace beyond all understanding, which comes at its maximum only to the man who has given up golf.

P. G. WODEHOUSE

....

If God wanted you to putt cross-handed, he would have made your left arm longer.

LEE TREVINO

....

I'm certainly not a saint out there on the golf course. In fact, far from it. Like when you make a three-putt and become upset. I take one step back and remember there are more important things going on in the world than golf.

BERNHARD LANGER, *THE ROUND OF MY LIFE*, 1998

Some of Hale Irwin's shots today were Godlike.

COLIN MONTGOMERIE, AFTER LOSING HIS RYDER CUP FOURSOMES AGAINST IRWIN AND WADKINS IN 1991

No power on earth will deter men from using a ball that will add to the length of their drive.

GOLF ILLUSTRATED MAGAZINE, DESCRIBING THE ADVENT OF THE HASKELL BALL IN 1901

This putting is wicked. It is sinful.

JAMES BRAID, COMPETING IN THE 1900 BRITISH OPEN AT
ST ANDREWS

Here's your headline for a picture of that: 'Casper to Knees:
Lord Says No!'

GEORGE ARCHER, TO REPORTERS AS RIVAL BILLY CASPER
MISSES A PUTT ON THE 18TH GREEN AT AUGUSTA TO TIE
HIM IN THE 1970 MASTERS

He [José Maria Olazabal] still has a putt to tie the hole. We can
still take the Ryder Cup home. It was disgusting! And Tom
Lehman calls himself a Man of God ...

AN IRATE SAM TORRANCE, DESCRIBING THE CLOSING SCENES
OF THE 1999 RYDER CUP AT BROOKLINE AS MEMBERS OF
THE USA TEAM, INCLUDING TOM LEHMAN, RAN ACROSS THE
PENULTIMATE GREEN TO CONGRATULATE JASON LEONARD

If you call on God to improve the results of a shot while it is
still in motion, you are using an outside agency and are subject
to appropriate penalties under the rules of golf.

HENRY LONGHURST

Some of us worship in churches, some in synagogues, some on
golf courses.

ADLAI STEVENSON II, AMERICAN POLITICIAN AND AUTHOR

Its fascinations have always been gratefully acknowledged, and not a few of its worthier practitioners have from time to time in prose and verse, rehearsed its praises.

ROBERT CLARK, 1875

They were real golfers, for real golf is a thing of the spirit, not of mere mechanical excellence of stroke.

P. G. WODEHOUSE

There but for the grace of God ...

HENRY LONGHURST'S IMMORTAL COMMENT ABOUT THE SHORT MISSED PUTT ON THE FINAL GREEN AT ST ANDREWS WHICH COST DOUG SANDERS THE 1970 BRITISH OPEN

I can sum it up like this: Thank God for the game of Golf.

ARNOLD PALMER

How do I combat it? Just pray a little bit, I suppose ...

MARK O'MEARA, 1998 MASTERS CHAMPION, ON THE DIFFICULTY OF PLAYING THE PAR-THREE 12TH AT AUGUSTA UNDER TOURNAMENT PRESSURE

....

No doubt these heathen gods, the very minute,
They knew the game would have delighted in it,
War, storms and thunder, all would have been off,
Mars, Jove and Neptune would have studied golf.

ANDREW CARNEGIE, SCOTTISH ESSAYIST, 1896

....

It was perceived as war paint but actually it was clay. It's a traditional Indian custom. You do it when you say a prayer to the powers that be for strength when you have something hard to do and need help. I perceive each game of golf to be like that, a long journey when there are a lot of obstacles to be overcome, both physically and emotionally.

NOTAH BEGAY III, A NATIVE AMERICAN INDIAN AND
PROFESSIONAL GOLFER, WHO WAS KNOWN DURING HIS
AMATEUR DAYS TO DAUB HIS CHEEKS WITH 'WAR PAINT'

I was driving like an idiot and putting like an angel.

KEN BOUSFIELD, DESCRIBING HIS SINGLES MATCH WITH THE
AMERICAN JAY HEBERT THAT ULTIMATELY WON THE RYDER
CUP AT LINDRICK IN 1957

When I come back in the next life, I want to come back as a golf pro's wife. She wakes up every morning at the crack of ten, and is faced by her first major decision of the day: whether to have breakfast in bed or in the hotel coffee shop.

DAN SYKES, US TOUR PROFESSIONAL

St Andrews is to the golfer what Mecca is to the Mohammedan. The comparison is apt in many respects. The Mohammedan turns his face towards Mecca when he prays. The golfer turns his thoughts towards St Andrews.

ROBERT BARCLAY, A BATCH OF GOLFING PAPERS, 1892

When a putter is waiting his turn to hole-out a putt of one or two feet in length, on which the match hangs at the last hole, it is of vital importance that he think of nothing At this supreme moment be ought studiously to fill his mind with vacancy. He must not even allow himself the consolations of religion. He must not prepare himself to accept the gloomy face of his partner and the derisive delight of his adversaries with Christian resignation should he miss.

SIR WALTER SIMPSON, *THE ART OF GOLF*, 1887

If I were a man I wouldn't have half a dozen Tom Collins's before going out to play golf, then let profanity substitute for proficiency on the golf course.

PATTY BERG, LEGENDARY WOMEN GOLF PROFESSIONAL, *LADIES' HOME JOURNAL*, 1945

God must watch over left-handers, because nobody else does.

FURMAN BISHER, *ATLANTA JOURNAL*, 1984

In his after-life this haphazard player, who taught himself and makes it his boast that he had only one lesson in his life, will probably come to wish that he had had more and that he had built his game on a sound foundation. These regrets are inevitable. The golf world is over-populated with persons who wish they had commenced to play in the proper way.

JAMES BRAID, *HOW TO PLAY GOLF*, 1901

Rich and poor alike are smitten with the fever;
Their business and religion to play;
And a man is scarcely deemed a true believer,
Unless he goes round at least a round a day.

A SCOTTISH VERSE, 1855

In my opinion, a man should never make excuses for himself at golf. It's like being disrespectful to Providence.

UNKNOWN SCOTTISH CADDIE, GOLFING MAGAZINE, 1894

By the shores of the Northern Sea lies a spacious territory of turf and bunker, with the joy and desire of all those who handle the club. Without profanity, one may call it the 'Holy Land of Golf'.

JOHN GEDDIE, ESSAYS AND REMINISCENCES, 1896

Nothing contributes more to the popularity of golf than its almost endless variety. No two courses are the same, even though they be similar in character; no two shots are alike, even though the same distance has to be accomplished.

JOHN L. LOW, *CONCERNING GOLF*, 1903

A good golf course makes you want to play so badly you hardly have time to change your shoes.

BEN CRENSHAW

This course is not like anything in Scotland or Ireland. It's like something in Mars.

DAVID FEHERTY, TALKING ABOUT THE OCEAN COURSE AT KIAWAH ISLAND SHORTLY BEFORE THE RYDER CUP WAS HELD THERE IN 1991

If you don't get goose bumps when you walk into this place [Augusta National] you don't have a pulse.

HAL SUTTON

The ideal golf course is one that will test all golfers equally according to their respective abilities, and at the same time give them an equal amount of pleasure.

W. HERBERT FOWLER, OLD-TIME GOLF COURSE ARCHITECT

Most of our inland courses are so bad that to the uninitiated observer the game must appear a very futile kind of sport. In many cases the lies are abominable, the putting greens so coarse that no finesse in the short game is possible and in nearly all it is heavy odds that you cannot get round the links in summer without losing several balls.

H. J. WHIGHAM, TALKING ABOUT THE STANDARD OF GOLF COURSES IN THE UNITED STATES, 1910

Augusta National is a young man's golf course, and you really need a young man's nerves to play on it.

JACK NICKLAUS

[Playing Augusta National] is like playing a Salvador Dali landscape. I expected a clock to fall out of the trees and hit me in the face.

DAVID FEHERTY

Bunkers have probably caused more joy and/or misery to the human race than any other subtle torturings of man's contriving.

H. MACNEILE DIXON, *GOLF AND HOW*, 1944

The pin placements weren't too tough, but whoever set them missed ten greens.

PROFESSIONAL GOLFER **LEONARD THOMPSON,** ON THE TRICKY PIN POSITIONS DURING THE FINAL ROUND OF THE GREATER GREENSBORO OPEN IN 1975

The attraction of the game of golf for many club players lies in the simple matter of escape and change – escape from the routine of work and home, and change from the inhibiting environment of factory or office. The attraction of the rolling green acres, the trees, the brooks, the smoothly tailored greens and the warmth of the club and of being part of the club, is compulsive.

PETER ALLISS

Pine Valley is the shrine of American golf because so many golfers are buried there.

ED SULLIVAN, FORMER US TALK SHOW HOST

On the golf course, a man may be the dogged victim of inexorable fate, be struck down by an appalling stroke of tragedy, become the hero of unbelievable melodrama, or the clown in a side-splitting comedy – any of these within a few hours, and all without having to bury a corpse or repair a tangled personality.

BOBBY JONES

The hazards and bumps on the course are there to offer a challenge to the skill, courage and philosophy of the player, who suffers no interference in his game except from nature. The geography of the course, the temper of the elements, the quality of his courage and the unevenness of his temperament are the obstacles to be overcome.

ROBERT HARRIS, *SIXTY YEARS OF GOLF*, 1953

Golf course architects make me sick. They can't play themselves, so they rig the courses so nobody else can play either.

SAM SNEAD

It is usually considered bad form to draw one's opponent's attention to some rare plant whilst he is actually playing a shot. The replacement of divots or other excavated turf is encouraged by members who have the good of the course at heart, though the principle of placing a divot over one's opponent's ball in the hope that it may be given up as lost is deplored, except in certain Continental centres.

H. MacNEILE DIXON, *GOLF AND HOW*, 1944

Anyone who criticizes a golf course is like a person invited to a house for dinner who, on leaving, tells the host that the food was lousy.

GARY PLAYER

Carnoustie Golf Club, Scotland: a good swamp, spoiled.

GARY PLAYER

Ever since the historic day when a visiting clergyman accomplished the feat of pulling a ball from the 10th tee at an angle of 225 degrees into the river that is the rightful receptacle for the 8th tee, the Stockbridge golf course has had 17 out of 18 holes that are punctuated with water hazards. The charming course itself lies in the flat of the sunken meadows which the Housatonic, in the few thousand years which are necessary for the proper preparation of a golf course, has obligingly eaten out of the high accompanying bluffs. The river, which goes wriggling on its way as though convulsed with merriment, is garnished with luxurious elms and willows, which occasionally deflect to the difficult putting greens the random slices of certain notorious amateurs.

OWEN JOHNSON, *EVEN THREES*, 1912

The skill that every player has can be seen at Augusta; it demands all the shots; nothing is taken away from you. If you have skill and imagination you can show it at Augusta.

DAVID DAVIES, BRITISH GOLF COLUMNIST

To me, the ground here is hallowed. The grass grows greener, the trees bloom better, there is even warmth to the rocks ... somehow or other the sun seems to shine on The Country Club (of Brookline, Massachusetts) more than any other place I have ever known.

FRANCIS OUIMET, ON THE COURSE ON WHICH HE WON THE US OPEN IN 1913

It is a wonderful tribute to the game or to the dottiness of the people who play it that for some people somewhere there is no such thing as an insurmountable obstacle, an unplayable course, the wrong time of the day or year.

ALISTAIR COOKE

The difference between golf in America and golf in England is that one is artificial and the other is natural.

H. J. WHIGHAM, *GOLF AND GOLFERS*, 1899

....

A golf course is the epitome of all that is purely transitory in the universe, a space not to dwell in, but to get over as quickly as possible.

JEAN GIRAUDO

....

The ardent golfer would play Mount Everest if somebody would put a flagstick on top.

PETE DYE, TOP US GOLF COURSE DESIGNER

Cursed be the hand that made these fatal holes.

WILLIAM SHAKESPEARE, *RICHARD III*

The Scots say that Nature itself dictated that golf should be played by the seashore. Rather, the Scots saw in the eroded sea coasts a cheap battleground on which they could whip their fellow men in a game based on the Calvinist doctrine that man is meant to suffer here below and never more than when he goes out to enjoy himself.

ALISTAIR COOKE

I knew it was a tough hole but I didn't think it could break your arm.

GUY WOLSTENHOLME, WHO SLIPPED AND FELL WHILE CLAMBERING DOWN A STEEP EMBANKMENT DURING AN AMATEUR TOURNAMENT

I can't tell you how many bunkers I have seen placed to catch shots that are already wayward. Hazards should be placed strategically to disrupt the line of play.

ALISTER MacKENZIE, OLD-TIME GOLF COURSE ARCHITECT, *THE GOOD DOCTOR RETURNS*

Sometimes a particular hole will cause a choke – a choke hole. Like the 18th at Cypress. It's like walking into a certain room in a big dark house when you were a kid – you get this fear that hits you.

DAVE MARR

If you moved Pebble Beach fifty miles inland, no one would have heard of it.

JIMMY DEMARET, 1950 US MASTERS CHAMPION

The winner, Severiano Ballesteros, chose not to use the course but preferred his own, which mainly consisted of hay fields, car parks, grandstands, dropping zones and even ladies' clothing.

COLIN McLAINE, CHAIRMAN OF THE OPEN CHAMPIONSHIP COMMITTEE, ROYAL LYTHAM, 1979

I'd like to see the fairways more narrow – then everybody would have to play from the rough, not just me.

SEVE BALLESTEROS

The man who doesn't feel emotionally stirred when he golfs at Pinehurst beneath those clear blue skies and with the pine fragrance in his nostrils is one who should be ruled out of golf for life.

BOBBY JONES

The real trick of golf course architecture is to lure the golfer into a false sense of security.

PETER DYE

Pebble Beach is Alcatraz with grass.

BOB HOPE, COMPETING IN THE CROSBY PRO-AM, 1952

The strategy of the golf course is the soul of the game. The spirit of golf is to dare a hazard, and by negotiating it reap a reward.

GEORGE C. THOMAS, JR, PIONEERING GOLF COURSE ARCHITECT

The good chip is like the good sand trap shot, it's your secret weapon. It allows you to whistle while you walk in the dark alleys of golf.

TOMMY BOLT

The difference between a sand trap and water is the difference between a car crash and an airplane crash. You have a chance of recovering from a car crash.

BOBBY JONES

There is no such thing as a misplaced bunker. Regardless of where a bunker may be, it is the business of the player to avoid it.

DONALD ROSS, LEGENDARY GOLF COURSE ARCHITECT

If your ball lands within a club length of a rattlesnake you are allowed to move the ball.

LOCAL SIGN EXPLAINING ONE PARTICULAR HAZARD AT THE GLEN CANYON COURSE IN ARIZONA

The object of a bunker or trap is not only to punish a physical mistake, to punish lack of control, but also to punish pride and egotism.

CHARLES BLAIR MACDONALD, DESIGNER OF THE NATIONAL GOLF CLUB, LONG ISLAND

A ball will always come to rest halfway down a hill, unless there is sand or water at the bottom.

HENRY BEARD, AMERICAN SATIRIST

St Andrews never impressed me at all. I wondered how it got such a reputation. The only reason could be on account of its age.

'WILD' BILL MEHLHORN, US RYDER CUP GOLFER

Golf is not a fair game, so why build a fair course?

PETER DYE

The Seven Deadly Sins of Architecture: greens that don't drain; greens that drain too much; greens too large for small shots; greens too small for large shots; greens too freakish for any shot; holes playing directly into the slopes of hills; holes requiring climbs to higher levels too suddenly.

A. W. TILLINGHAST, LEGENDARY GOLF COURSE DESIGNER

A good golf course is like good music. It does not necessarily appeal the first time one plays it.

ALISTER MACKENZIE, DESIGNER OF AUGUSTA NATIONAL, GEORGIA

If you have an ego of any sort, this course will take it and shove it down your throat.

TOM WATSON, ON AUGUSTA NATIONAL

There are many bad long courses and many very good short courses, and length has very little to do with merit.

HARRY S. COLT, BRITISH GOLF COURSE ARCHITECT OF THE 1920S

Prestwick has always taken a leading part in the settlement of important professional matches. The links are as eminently adapted in every way for these contests, and provide as good a test of Golf, as the best links in the kingdom. There is no living golfer of repute among the professionals who has not played in important matches over the ground.

J. McBAIN, *GOLF*, 1891

I don't think I've ever played there.

SANDY LYLE, WHEN ASKED ABOUT THE THEN PROMISING AMATEUR, TIGER WOODS

I feel like I just fought a war.

HAL SUTTON, AFTER A BATTLING FIRST-ROUND 73 AT CARNOUSTIE IN THE 1999 BRITISH OPEN

Hitting the fairways is like driving the ball through the door of my hotel bedroom.

GREG NORMAN, EXPLAINING THE DIFFICULTY OF PLAYING
CARNOUSTIE DURING THE 1999 BRITISH OPEN

I've been around golf courses all my life. When I get out on that green carpet called a fairway and manage to poke the ball right down the middle, my surroundings look like a touch of heaven on earth.

JIMMY DEMARET

Golf architects, knowing full well the simple weaknesses of all players, have with diabolical cunning inserted, as it were, these mantraps just where they can be sure to ensnare the greatest number of victims.

H. MacNEILE DIXON, ON BUNKERS, *GOLF AND HOW*, 1944

In 1895, a newspaperman called Tom Bendelow resigned from his job at the *New York Herald* and turned his hand to golf course design. His sole qualification when he started was that he spoke with a convincing Scottish accent. Working for Spalding as a 'design-consultant', his golf courses were labelled descriptively as 'Sunday Specials' because of the time it took him to design them. With few clients knowledgeable enough about golf to question his methods, Bendelow would confidently walk around the proposed site, plant one stick for the tee, another for the fairway bunker, and mark the green with a pile of stones. He would repeat this same process nine, twelve or eighteen times, depending on the amount of holes required. The only things left to chance were the greens – whether square or round.

A. J. Dalconan, *Golf:The History of the Royal & Ancient Game*, 1995

[Robert Trent] Jones has so many doglegs on this course, he must have laid it out in a kennel.

Bob Rosburg, talking about Hazeltine National, site of the 1970 US Open, after shooting 79 in the first round

Some might say it's an easy shot. Well, it might be today, but there's this little sign that goes up that says: 'US Open'.

USGA President, Judy Bell, on Congressional's 190-yard, par-three 18th hole, 1998

I love Merion, and I don't even know her last name.

Lee Trevino, after winning the 1971 US Open at Merion Golf Club

We are all aware that one cannot make a silk purse out of a sow's ear, or a proper links out of an old park, or fields of good inland pasture.

Tom Simpson, golf course designer, 1925

It is a hole too far.

The Bournemouth Echo, responding to a planned putting hole designed by Damien Hirst. The hole involved hitting the ball into the middle of two buttocks named 'Hairy Hills'.

Golf may be played anywhere – that is, anywhere where there is room, but the quality of golf will depend upon the kind of place it is played on, and the manner in which the ground is laid out and kept.

GARDEN G. SMITH, WRITER, OUTLINING THE BASIC PRINCIPLES OF GOLF COURSE DESIGN, 1898

All truly great golf courses have an almost supernatural finishing hole, by way of separating the chokers from the strokers.

CHARLES PRICE

Providence obviously designed this for a golf course.

GENERAL MONCRIEFFE, ON THE SPOT CHOSEN FOR THE 'NEW' ROYAL NORTH DEVON GOLF CLUB IN BIDEFORD, 1863. THE FAMED WESTWARD HO IS NOW THE OLDEST GOLF COURSE IN ENGLAND

Great golf courses should have at least one silly hole.

FRANK HANNIGAN, FORMER USGA DIRECTOR

You gotta sneak up on these holes. If you clamber and clank up on 'em, they're liable to turn around and bite you.

SAM SNEAD, TALKING ABOUT OAKMONT COUNTRY CLUB, PENNSYLVANIA

Cypress Point is the Sistine Chapel of golf.

SANDY TATUM, FORMER USGA PRESIDENT

Not necessarily. It simply seems to require more skill than I have at the moment.

BEN HOGAN, ASKED WHETHER THE PAR-THREE 12TH HOLE
AT AUGUSTA NATIONAL WAS IMPOSSIBLE IN HIGH WINDS

A great golf hole is one which puts a question mark into the player's mind when he arrives on the tee to play it.

MACKENZIE ROSS, BRITISH COURSE ARCHITECT

Golf on the Continent is not necessarily played à l'anglais ou l'écossais and foreign customs may prevail. It is not unusual to see pater-familias, mater-familias and all the little familiasses marching together with their French poodle, clipped à la privet hedge, in tow down to the links.

H. MACNEILE DIXON, GOLF AND HOW, 1944

To play golf properly there is needed a very large expanse of uncultivated soil, which is not too much broken up by hills. A few knolls and gulleys more or less assist to make the game more interesting. In Scotland it is played generally upon the east coast, where the links are most extensive. Having selected a field, the first thing necessary is to dig a small hole, perhaps one foot or two feet deep and about four inches in diameter. Beginning with this hole a circle is devised that includes substantially the whole of the links. About once in 500 yards of this circle another hole is dug. If the grounds selected cannot include so large a circle as this, the holes may be put at as short a distance as 100 yards from each other; but the best game is played when the field is large enough to include holes at a distance of 500 yards apart.

THE PHILADELPHIA TIMES, EXPLAINING TO THE AMERICAN
PUBLIC WHAT CONSTITUTES A GOOD GOLF COURSE, 1889

The greens are harder than a whore's heart.

SAM SNEAD, ON US OPEN VENUE WINGED FOOT GOLF
CLUB, NEW YORK

It's *Star Wars* golf. The place was designed by Darth Vader.

BEN CRENSHAW, TALKING ABOUT THE TOURNAMENT
PLAYERS CLUB AT SAWGRASS, FLORIDA

When you get to your ball, you're too tired to hit it.

ROBYN DUMMETT, AMERICAN TOUR PRO, ON THE APPARENT
DIFFICULTY OF SPEIDEL GOLF CLUB, WEST VIRGINIA

Tell me, do you chaps actually play this hole – or just photograph it?

EUSTACE STOREY, BRITISH AMATEUR, ON THE EXCESSIVELY
TIGHT, TREE-LINED FAIRWAYS AT PINE VALLEY, NEW JERSEY,
1920s

In all my travels, I do not think I have seen a more beautiful landscape. This is as thrilling as Versailles or Fontainebleau.

LOWELL THOMAS, AMERICAN RADIO HOST, ON PINE
VALLEY, 1950s

The man who doesn't feel emotionally stirred when he golfs at Pinehurst ... should be ruled out of golf for life.

TOMMY ARMOUR, 1959

I'm glad to have brought this monster to its knees.

BEN HOGAN, AFTER WINNING THE US OPEN AT MERION,
1951

Golf is like a love affair: If you don't take it seriously, it's not fun; if you do take it seriously, it breaks your heart.

ARNOLD DALY

In almost all other games you pit yourself against a moral foe; in golf it is yourself against the world: no human being stays your progress as you drive your ball over the face of the globe.

ARNOLD HAULTAIN, *THE MYSTERY OF GOLF*, 1910

Golf is not one of those occupations in which you soon learn your level. There is no shape nor size of body, no awkwardness nor ungainliness, which puts good golf beyond one's reach. There are good golfers with spectacles, with one eye, with one leg, even with one arm. None but the absolutely blind need despair. It is not the youthful tyro alone who has cause to hope. Beginners in middle age have become great, and, more wonderful still, after years of patient duffering, there may be a rift in the clouds. Some pet vice which has been clung to as a virtue

87

may be abandoned, and the fifth-class player burst upon the world as a medal winner. In golf, whilst there is life there is hope.

SIR WALTER SIMPSON, *THE ART OF GOLF*, 1887

Golf is an indispensable adjunct to high civilization.

ANDREW CARNEGIE, AMERICAN INDUSTRIALIST AND PHILANTHROPIST WHO MADE A GIFT OF $200,000 TO YALE UNIVERSITY TO BUILD A GOLF COURSE

Golf is a good walk spoiled.

MARK TWAIN

Golf is essentially an exercise in masochism conducted out-of-doors; it affords opportunity for a certain swank, it induces a sense of kinship in its victims, and it forces them to breathe fresh air, but it is, at bottom, an elaborate and addictive rite calculated to drive them crazy for hours on end and send them straight to the whisky bottle after that.

PAUL O'NEIL

Golf is the Esperanto of sport. All over the world golfers talk the same language – much of it nonsense and much unprintable – endure the same frustrations, discover the same infallible secretsof putting, share the same illusory joys.

HENRY LONGHURST

Golf is a game of the people. It is played by the Common Man as a sport and a relaxation from the worries of life rather than used as an exhibition for onlookers, to which it is not suited.

ROBERT HARRIS, *SIXTY YEARS OF GOLF*, 1953

Golf is an easy game ... It's just hard to play.

ANON.

Golf is more exacting than racing, cards, speculation or matrimony.

ARNOLD HAULTAIN, *THE MYSTERY OF GOLF*, 1910

Golf is the hardest game in the world. There's no way you can ever get it. Just when you think you do, the game jumps up and puts you in your place.

BEN CRENSHAW

Golf gives no margin: either you win or you fail. You cannot hedge; you cannot bluff; you cannot give a stop order. One chance is given you, and you hit or miss. There is nothing more rigid in life. And it is this ultra and extreme rigidity that makes golf so intensely interesting.

ARNOLD HAULTAIN, *THE MYSTERY OF GOLF*, 1910

Golf is the cruellest of sports. Like life, it's unfair. It's a harlot, a trollop. It leads you on. It never lives up to its promises. It's not a sport, it's bondage. An obsession. A boulevard of broken dreams. It plays with men. And runs off with the butcher.

JIM MURRAY, AMERICAN SPORTSWRITER

Golf is 90 per cent inspiration and 10 per cent perspiration.

JOHNNY MILLER

Golf is like love. One day you think you're too old, and the next you can't wait to do it again.

ROBERTO DE VINCENZO, 1967 BRITISH OPEN CHAMPION

Golf is 20 per cent mechanics and technique. The other 80 per cent is philosophy, humour, tragedy, romance, melodrama, companionship, camaraderie, cussedness, and conversation.

GRANTLAND RICE, *AMERICAN GOLFER* MAGAZINE, 1920

Golf is a non-violent game, played violently from within.

BOB TOSKI

Golf is a day spent in a round of strenuous idleness.

WILLIAM WORDSWORTH, ENGLISH POET

Golf is a game in which perfection stays just out of reach.

BETSY RAWLS, AMERICAN PROFESSIONAL

Golf is typical capitalist lunacy.

GEORGE BERNARD SHAW

Golf is not a game of great shots. It's a game of the most misses. The people who win make the smallest mistakes.

GENE LITTLER

Golf is not a game of good shots. It's a game of bad shots.

BEN HOGAN

Golf is a game that is measured in yards, but the difference between a hit and a miss is calipered in micro-millimeters.

TONY LEMA

Playing golf is just like going to a strip club. You're all revved up, ready to go. But three hours later, you're depressed, plastered, and most of your balls are missing.

JAMES CLARK, AMERICAN WRITER AND HUMORIST

Golf is a game where guts, stick-to-it-iveness and blind devotion will always net you absolutely nothing but an ulcer.

TOMMY BOLT

Golf is a game whose aim is to hit a very small ball into an even smaller hole, with weapons singularly ill-designed for the purpose.

SIR WINSTON CHURCHILL

Golf is based on honesty. Where else would someone admit to a seven on an easy par three?

JIMMY DEMARET

Golf is a game where the ball always lies poorly and the player always lies well.

POPULAR AMERICAN SAYING

Golf is a most difficult game to describe. I should liken it, in some respects, to billiards on a grand scale, except that the balls have to be put into holes instead of pockets; that they have to be struck with the side instead of with the end of a club, and that there is no such thing as cannoning.

W. H. G. KINGSTON, *ERNEST BRACEBRIDGE, OR SCHOOLBOY DAYS*, 1860

Golf is life. If you can't take golf, you can't take life.

POPULAR AMERICAN SAYING

Golf is neither a microcosm of nor a metaphor for life. It is a sport, a bloodless sport if you don't count ulcers.

DICK SCHAAP, AMERICAN SPORTS JOURNALIST AND BROADCASTER

Golf is a game in which you yell 'fore', shoot six and write down five.

PAUL HARVEY, AMERICAN RADIO BROADCASTER

A Royal & Very Ancient Game

In prehistoric times, cavemen had a custom of beating the ground with clubs and uttering spine-chilling cries. Anthropologists call this a form of primitive self-expression. When modern men go through the same ritual, they call it golf.

ANON.

An expert player will send the ball an amazing distance at one stroke, and each player follows his ball upon an open heath, and he who strikes it in fewest strokes into a hole wins the game.

WILLIAM GUTHRIE, 1774

Perth stands in the middle of a beautiful green about an English mile in length, and divides it into two, called the north and south Inches, where the citizens for ages have exercised themselves during the spring and autumnal seasons with golf-clubs and balls. This pastime is interrupted during the summer-season by the luxuriancy of the grass, which affords rich pasture for the milch-cows belonging to the inhabitants.

JAMES CANT, THE MUSES THRENODIE, DESCRIBING GOLF IN THE 'FAIR CITY' OF PERTH, 1774

There was not much chance of the game becoming popular. There was not enough activity in it to please them. It was not to be compared for a moment with cricket or rackets or football or even hockey.

W. H. G. KINGSTON, *ERNEST BRACEBRIDGE, OR SCHOOLBOY DAYS*, 1860

....

Ever since golf began – Scottish historians have settled on the year 1100 as a reasonable date of birth – the game has been an enigma.

HERBERT WARREN WIND

....

Golf is a game with a shady past. Its actual birth is shrouded in mystery. No one is quite certain when or where it drew its first tortured breath. Golf cannot point to a legal father, such as baseball in the case of Abner Doubleday or basketball in the case of Dr James A. Naismith. In fact, there is a question that golf was ever born at all. As some scientists contend in regard to man himself, the game may have just evolved.

WILL GRIMSLEY, *GOLF: ITS HISTORY, PEOPLE AND EVENTS*, 1966

No person or persons shall be permitted to play at Golf over the Castlehill without a runner before to forewarn passengers, passing or repassing to keep out of harm's way. And the Magistrats are powered at any time to stop all idle persons from Grazing on the Green to the prejudice of the pasture grounds.

NORTH BERWICK COUNCIL MINUTE, 21 MARCH 1775

The youths in this country are very manly in their exercises and amusements. Strength and agility seems to be most their attention. The insignificant pastimes of marbles, tops, etc., they are totally unacquainted with. The diversion which is peculiar to Scotland, and in which all ages find great pleasure, is golf. The art consists in striking the ball with this instrument, into a hole in the ground, in a smaller number of strokes than your adversary. This game has the superiority of cricket and tennis, in being less violent and dangerous; but in point of dexterity and amusement, by no means to be compared with them. However, I am informed that some skill and nicety are necessary to strike the ball to the proposed distance and no further, and that in this there is a considerable difference in players. It requires no great exertion and strength, and all ranks and ages play at it. They instruct their children in it, as soon as they can run alone, and grey hairs boast their execution.

EDWARD TOPHAM, *LETTERS FROM EDINBURGH*, 1776

Golf is an exercise which is much used by the Gentlemen of Scotland. A large common in which there are several little holes is chosen for the purpose. It is played with little leather balls stuffed with feathers and sticks ... He who puts a ball into a given number of holes, with the fewest strokes, gets the game. The late Dr McKenzie, author of the essay on Health and Long Life, used to say that a man would live ten years the longer for using this exercise once or twice a week.

BENJAMIN RUSH, WHO, AMONG OTHERS, SIGNED THE
AMERICAN DECLARATION OF INDEPENDENCE

May your balls, as they fly and whiz through the air
Knock down the blue devils, dull sorrow and care
May your health be preserved, with strength active and bold
Long traverse the green, and forget to grow old.

HENRY CALLENDER, POET AND PAST CAPTAIN OF ROYAL
BLACKHEATH GOLF CLUB IN 1790, 1801 AND 1807

Among others, I was shown one particular set of golfers, the youngest of whom was turned of four-score [80]. They were all gentlemen of independent fortunes, who had amused them-selves with this pastime for the best part of a century without having ever felt the least alarm from sickness or disgust; and they never went to bed without having each the best part of a gallon of claret in his belly.

TOBIAS SMOLLETT, *THE EXPEDITION OF HUMPHRY CLINKER*,
1771

I sometimes wonder if he shouldn't stop reading so much about golf history and start making some.

DAVE MARR

There never was a game like the old Scottish Game.
That's played twixt the hole and the tee;
You may roam the world o'er but the game at your door,
Is the very best game you will see.

ANON., 1845

Golf is widely referred to as the Royal and Ancient Game – Ancient because of the five hundred years it has been played in one form or another, and Royal because of its equally long association with the Kings and Queens of Scotland. But while successive Scottish monarchs ratified Acts which forbade their subjects to play golf, they had few inhibitions about playing the game themselves.

MARK MCKENNA

[His] entire nature was bent on being a golfer. It is yet told on the links how Allan would rise betimes and, with shirt sleeves rolled up for better muscular play, start alone for practice across the deserted links, still wet with early dew. Allan has improved in his day on the old theories of golf and to him are owing many of the improved methods and styles of the present game.

THE DUNDEE ADVERTISER ON GOLF'S FIRST PROFESSIONAL,
ALLAN ROBERTSON, 1859

This all our life we frolik and gay,
And instead of court revels we merrily play,
At Trap, at Rules, and at Barley-break run,
At Goff and at Foot-Ball, and when we have done,
These innocent sports, we'll laugh and lie down.

THOMAS SHADWELL, ENGLISH PLAYWRIGHT, C.1680

It is decreeted and ordained ... that the Fute-ball and Golfe be utterly cryed downe, and not to be used. And as tuitching the Futeball and the Golfe, to be punished by the Barronniss un-law.

JAMES II OF SCOTLAND, BANNING GOLF FOR THE FIRST
TIME IN 1457. IT SEEMED THAT THE SCOTS WERE
NEGLECTING THEIR ARCHERY PRACTICE.

It is statute and ordained that in na place of the Realme there be used Fute-ball, Golfe or uther sik unproffitable sportes.

JAMES IV OF SCOTLAND, BANNING GOLF IN 1491

[The King's] subjects be very glad. I thank God to be busy with the golf, for they take it for pastime; my heart is very good to it.

QUEEN CATHERINE, IN A LETTER TO CARDINAL WOLSEY IN 1513, WHEN HENRY VIII WAS AWAY INVADING FRANCE

Tam Arte Quam Marte: As much by skill as by strength.

THE CLUB MOTTO OF ROYAL TROON GOLF CLUB IN SCOTLAND

Of this diversion the Scots are so fond, that, when the weather will permit, you may see a multitude of all ranks, from the senator of justice to the lowest tradesman, mingled together, in their shirts, and following the balls with the utmost eagerness.

TOBIAS SMOLLETT, ON THE GROWING POPULARITY OF GOLF, 1771

Walter Hay, goldsmith, accusit for playing at the boulis and golf upoun Sundaye in the tyme of the sermon.

TOWN RECORDS OF ELGIN, 1596. PUNISHMENT FOR SUCH A CRIME COULD MEAN SPENDING A WEEK IN THE STOCKS — A NOT INCONSIDERABLE PENALTY

There shall be no public playing permitted on the Sabbath days such as playing at bowls, at the penny stone, archery, golf ...

And if any be found playing publicly in a yard or in fields upon the Sabbath day from morning until evening they shall pay 20 shillings to the poor and also make their public repentance from the pulpit.

THE SOUTH LEITH KIRK SESSION (EDINBURGH), FEBRUARY 1610

This man by his skill in many exercises, particularly the golf, and by gentlemanly behaviour, was admitted to the company of his superiors, which elated his mind.

DR CARLYLE, EIGHTEENTH-CENTURY ESSAYIST, DESCRIBING CAPTAIN PORTEOUS JOINING THE FLEDGELING HONOURABLE COMPANY OF EDINBURGH GOLFERS

The early development of Royal North Devon was typical of what was later to become a common process in Victorian England. The first clubhouse was nothing more than a mobile bathers' changing-room. On competition days it was stocked with food and drinks and physically dragged to the course by the members. This was replaced in turn by a bell-tent, a marquee and a small wooden hut with corrugated tin roof. During these early years, everything about the club was rough and ready; the wooden hut was only big enough to accommodate an old table, chairs and small bar, while the members' hickory clubs were placed upon the rafters for safe-keeping.

A. J. DALCONEN, GOLF: THE HISTORY OF THE ROYAL & ANCIENT GAME, 1995

*Lurking in the churchyard while golf was in progress [he was hit] under his
left lung [by] ane deidlie straik.*

LOCAL RECORDS REPORTING THE DEATH OF THOMAS
CHATTO OF KELSO IN 1632. IT SEEMS HE HAD BEEN HIT IN
THE CHEST BY A GOLF BALL.

A golfer who has never made for sale any golf clubs, balls, or
any articles connected with the game, who had never carried
clubs for hire after attaining the age of fifteen years, and who
has not carried clubs for hire at any time within six years of the
date on which the competition begins each year: who has never
received any consideration for playing in a match or for giving
lessons in the game. and who, for a period of five years prior to
the 1st of September. 1886, has never received a money prize in
an open [championship] competition.

ROYAL LIVERPOOL GOLF CLUB, DEFINING THE DIFFERENCE
BETWEEN AN AMATEUR AND PROFESSIONAL GOLFER — THE
FIRST TIME ANY SUCH RULING WAS MADE

A great match of golf was played yesterday and excited the
ambition of the crack players in the land ... The game made
much progress, and it became evident to the various tyrol that
the tug of war would be between the champions of Prestwick
[Morris] and Musselburgh [Park]. Morris was the favourite as
much on the account of his deservedly great reputation as much
as the advantage he enjoyed traversing his own ground.

THE AYR ADVERTISER, REPORTING ON THE VERY FIRST
BRITISH OPEN CHAMPIONSHIP AT PRESTWICK, 1860

The origin of the freak match, like the origin of golf itself is, unhappily, lost in antiquity. The first we call to mind was one in which a Sandwich golfer, with a champagne bottle as his only club, beat a fellow member playing with a full set of clubs in a match over the Royal St George's green. The latter, we believe, was a scratch player.

C. W. LIMOUZIN, 1913

Although the vast majority of Anglo-Cingalese golf from love of the game, a certain number of exiles play from quite another motive. Afraid of developing a 'liver' – a complaint from which few expatriate Britons are exempt – they have to take active exercise, and golf, being best suited to their requirements, is seized upon as a means towards an end.

GEORGE CECIL, ON THE PROBLEMS OF PLAYING GOLF IN CEYLON IN 1912

Up until the mid-eighteenth century, golf was still a relatively classless game. The street urchin with his bent stick and supply of pebbles was as common a sight on the links as the wealthy merchant with his long-nose woods and stock of feather balls.

A. J. DALCONEN, GOLF: THE HISTORY OF THE ROYAL & ANCIENT GAME, 1995

Far and Sure.

THE MOTTO OF THE ROYAL & ANCIENT GOLF CLUB OF ST ANDREWS

To write the history of golf as it should be done, a young man must do it, and he will be so ancient before he finishes the toil that he will scarce see the flag on the short hole at St Andrews from the tee.

ROBERT BROWNING, *A HISTORY OF GOLF*, 1955

Scarcely had the minstrels ceased to serenade them, when we find Montrose at his clubs and balls again.

SCOTTISH RECORDS, 10 NOVEMBER 1629, DESCRIBING HOW THE DUKE OF MONTROSE SPENT HIS HONEYMOON

The squalls, though short, were heavy; at the first symptoms of dropping there was a cry of 'Here it comes' and the whole four-somes with their caddies, skeddaddled for the nearest bunker, and stretched at full length under the ledge till the fury had passed away. In the distance as the storm drove to leeward, fellows who were not near bunkers made for big rushes, which with the help of an umbrella, don't form bad shelter; others regardless of squalls, took the opportunity of passing their leaders. On the eleventh, the rain which had before come at intervals, gave up and came down regular; the squalls ceased as the gale took up the blowing all to itself.

NEWSPAPER REPORT, AUGUST 1874

The basic urge in all players ... the urge that is the fatal fasci-nation of the game ... is hitting the ball out of sight.

GEORGE FULLERTON CARNEGIE OF PITARROW, 1813

The match started amidst the greatest enthusiasm. The weather had cleared up, but the wind blew pretty strong from the south-west. Each party had its own tail of supporters, those for the Musselburgh men predominating – for which, of course, the proximity of that place to North Berwick might account. They were led by Gourlay, the ball-maker. I never saw a match where such vehement party spirit was displayed. So great was the keenness and the anxiety to see whose ball had the best lie, that no sooner were the shots played than off the whole crowd ran, helter-skelter; and as one or the other lay best, so demonstrations were made by each party. Sir David Baird was umpire, and a splendid one he made. He was very tall and so commanded a good view of the field; but it took all his firmness to keep even tolerable order.

H. THOMAS PETER, DESCRIBING THE ACTION IN A £400 CHALLENGE MATCH BETWEEN TOM MORRIS AND ALLAN ROBERTSON OF ST ANDREWS AND THE DUNN BROTHERS OF MUSSELBURGH IN 1849

It may be said especially that mankind has always displayed a uniform craving for the pastime of hitting a ball with a stick. With the savage races, an enemy's head has taken the place of the ball, but the principle is still the same.

SCOTIA ON GOLF, 1886

Up to this time golf has made little way in the United States. It is occasionally played in Canada, although even there it has not assumed the importance of a regular department of sports. It is a game that demands the utmost physical development upon the part of the player as well as a considerable amount of skill, and it arouses the interest only of those who go into sports for the love of action. No man should attempt to play golf who has not good legs to run with and good arms to throw with, as well as a modicum of brain power to direct his play.

THE PHILADELPHIA TIMES, 1889

Garrick had built a handsome temple, with a statue of Shakespeare in it, in his lower garden on the banks of the Thames, which was separated from the upper one by a high road, under which there was an archway which united the two gardens. Having observed a green mound in the garden opposite the archway, I said to our landlord, that while the servants were preparing the collation in the temple I would surprise him with a stroke at the golf, as I should drive the ball through his archway into the Thames once in three strokes. I had measured the distance with my eye in walking about the garden, and, accordingly, at the second stroke, made the ball alight in the mouth of the gateway and roll down the green slope into the river. This was so dextrous that he was quite surprised, and begged the club of me by which such a feat had been performed.

ALEXANDER CARLYLE, 1860

Golf was rendered expensive in those days, not by the clubs, which were cheaper then than now, but by the balls. Their prime cost was high, and their durability not great. On a wet day, for example, a ball soon became soaked, soft and flabby; so that a new one had to be used at every hole in a match of any importance. Or, on the other hand, a 'top' by an iron in a bunker might cut it through. This I have frequently seen occur.

H. THOMAS PETER, GOLFING REMINISCENCES BY AN OLD HAND, 1890

At the beginning of play each player places his ball at the edge of a hole which has been designated as a starting point. When the word has been given to start he bats his ball as accurately as possible towards the next hole which is either 100 or 500 yards distant. As soon as it is started in the air he runs forward in the direction which the ball has taken, and his servant, who is called a 'caddy', runs after him with all the other nine tools in his arms. If the player is expert or lucky he bats the ball so that it falls within a few feet or inches even of the next hole in the circle. His purpose is to put the ball in the next hole, spoon it out and drive it forward to the next further one before his opponent can accomplish the same end.

THE PHILADELPHIA TIMES, OFFERING A SIMPLE GUIDE TO GOLF
FOR THE AMERICAN PUBLIC, 1889

Society is as prone to fads as are the sparks to fly upward. And the latest in outdoor fads is golf. Tennis, archery and polo have each had their turn, and golf is now coming in to replace them in the fickle minds of the Four Hundred. Without being as violent as tennis or polo, the ancient Scottish game furnishes more exercise than either archery or croquet and seems to find favour with those lovers of outdoor sports who are too stout, too old or too lazy to enjoy any of the severer games.

THE NEW YORK TIMES, DESCRIBING HOW HIGH SOCIETY IN
THE LONG ISLAND AREA TOOK TO GOLF IN 1894

When I learn that your club – the oldest in the country – is only twenty years old, and realize that I have been playing golf since 1896, I am surprised. I would, in respect to any other matter, feel very much discouraged at having attained in so long a time so little excellence. But golf is different from other games.

PRESIDENT TAFT, FROM A 1908 SPEECH HONOURING THE
20TH ANNIVERSARY OF THE ST ANDREWS CLUB, NEW
YORK

The total number of men and women who play golf is greater than the total number of men and women who watch and play baseball. Golf is becoming a national game, because both men and women can play. Baseball has its devotees only in the masculine ranks. Women can watch the game, but few can either understand or play it.

THE CLEVELAND PLAIN DEALER, 1900

As these six rounds came to 662 strokes, Capt. Molesworth played a seventh round, which he did in 104 strokes. Thus doing six rounds in one day, without counting the first round, in 646 strokes, winning by 14 strokes upon the six rounds; walked back, and reached home at twenty minutes to seven p.m. The question arises whether Captain Molesworth, having played six rounds in two strokes over the number, was entitled to play another round. Capt. Molesworth's backers say that the match was to play six rounds in one day between the hours of daylight and dark: and, therefore, it did not matter how many rounds he played, if six rounds were played in under 660 strokes, and that he was entitled to leave out the first or any other round, so long as six whole rounds were done under the number. The other side contended that, as six rounds were played, and the number of strokes taken was over 660, the match was lost. A case will be drawn, and the matter referred.

THE FIELD, REPORTING THE LEGAL IMPLICATIONS RESULTING FROM A CONTROVERSIAL GOLF MATCH AT ROYAL NORTH DEVON, SEPTEMBER 1877

Ladies on the Links

The lady golfer is a distinct genus, belonging to the order of Amazonae or athletic women.

AMY BENNET PASCOE, *GOLF AND GOLFERS*, 1899

With golf links in every neighbourhood, there is no reason why the middle-aged woman should fasten herself in the rocking chair and consent to be regarded by the youngsters around her as antiquated at forty-five. Instead of that, with firm tread, she can with her golfing club, follow her ball from link to link, renewing her beauty and youth by exercise in the open air.

JOHN GILMER SPEED, *THE LADIES HOME JOURNAL*, 1894

When you're that young and everything is so new, you don't fear failure. If she knocks her putts by, she just makes them coming back.

NANCY LOPEZ, ON RISING STAR SE RI PAK AFTER THE 1998 LPGA CHAMPIONSHIP

Ladies, I have a message for you. The members request that you do not shelter in front of the window, you are obscuring the view.

REQUEST BY A STEWARD OF THE ROYAL & ANCIENT GOLF CLUB OF ST ANDREWS DURING THE 1908 BRITISH LADIES CHAMPIONSHIP. BARRED FROM ENTERING THE HALLOWED PORTALS OF THE CLUBHOUSE, SOME COMPETITORS ATTEMPTED TO GAIN SOME RESPITE FROM A MAJOR DOWNPOUR. TODAY, WOMEN GOLFERS ARE STILL BANNED FROM ENTERING THE R&A

Golf, I have been told, is physically a better game for our sex than any other, as it exercises a greater number of muscles without fear of over-exertion or strain.

ISSETTE PEARSON, 1899

It really came home to me when one of my best mates thought I was dead because she saw my picture on the front page of the Daily Mirror. She was in the airport and her heart stopped. She thought, 'Laura's killed herself in that bloody car.' [Davies had recently bought a top-of-the-range BMW 850.] Then she read the story and laughed her socks off. What I find annoying is not that I made the front pages for that, it's more to do with how little space you get when you win two Major championships as I've done this year. If Monty or Faldo had won two Majors in 1996, they'd be royalty by now.

LAURA DAVIES, ON THE DIFFERENCE IN PRESS COVERAGE BETWEEN THE MEN'S TOUR AND THE WOMEN'S TOUR

A world without women would be worse than a world without flowers, and therefore it is every woman's duty to cultivate grace and comeliness. Let her play Golf to her heart's content, being assured that both grace and comeliness will be her portion.

LETTER TO THE EDITOR OF *GOLF MAGAZINE*, 1891

Women are admitted to play on the course only on sufferance and must at all times give way to [male] members

A NOTICE WHICH HUNG IN THE LUNCHEON ROOM AT ROYAL ST GEORGE'S GOLF CLUB, KENT, FROM 1902 TO 1927

It is to their presence as spectators that the most serious objection must be taken. If they could abstain from talking while you are playing, and if the shadow of their dresses would not flicker on the putting green while you are holing out, other objections might perhaps be waived ... If they volunteer to score, they may, and probably will score wrong (not in your favour you may be sure), yet you cannot contradict them.

LORD MONCREIFF, *GOLF*, 1890

Constitutionally and physically women are unfitted for golf. They will never last through two rounds of a long course in a day. Nor can they ever hope to defy the wind and weather encountered on our best links even in spring and summer. Temperamentally the strain will be too great for them.

LORD WELLWOOD, 1890

We should be allowed to wear shorts. God Almighty, women are allowed to wear them [on the LPGA Tour], and we've got better legs than they do.

GREG NORMAN

Golf humanizes women, humbles their haughty natures, tends, in short, to knock out of their systems a certain modicum of the superciliousness, that swank, which makes wooing a tough proposition for the diffident male.

HORACE HUTCHINSON, 1899

....

Women playing golf in trousers must take their trousers off before entering the clubhouse.

A SHORT-LIVED NOTICE POSTED AT ROYAL ST GEORGE'S GOLF CLUB IN THE LATE 1920S

....

During the last three holes of the 1919 US Open, which The Haig [Walter Hagen] won for the second time, he smiled at a pretty girl on the 16th tee, struck up a conversation with her on the 17th fairway, and made a date with her as he walked off the 18th green. After The Haig, nobody would take golf too seriously.

CHARLES PRICE, AMERICAN GOLF WRITER AND AUTHOR

I may not be the prettiest girl in the world, but I'd like to see Bo Derek rate a '10' after playing 18 holes in 100-degree heat.

JAN STEPHENSON, AUSTRALIAN PROFESSIONAL, ON HEARING SHE RATED A '6' IN THE *SAN JOSÉ MERCURY NEWS*, 1981

They've got the wrong person playing Wonder Woman on television.

JUDY RANKIN, ON THE RISE AND RISE OF NANCY LOPEZ IN THE LATE 1970S

After seeing Amy Alcott in the Women's US Open on TV, I was impressed with how she kissed her caddie when she won. My next move is to fire my caddie and find me one I can kiss.

LOU GRAHAM, 1975 US OPEN WINNER

I guess I'm not a professional's professional. I think I'd rather go to the dentist than play a practice round.

LAURA DAVIES

Look like a woman, but play like a man.

JAN STEPHENSON, ON THE PERFECT GOLFER, 1981

You trying to ask me do I wear girdles and bras and the rest of that junk? What do you think I am? A sissy?

BABE ZAHARIAS, LEGENDARY AMERICAN GOLFER

I noticed a lady in the clubhouse at the weekend. I urge the Secretary to see that this does not happen again.

ENTRY IN THE MEMBERS' COMPLAINT BOOK AT WORCESTERSHIRE GOLF CLUB, 1881

I can beat any two players in this tournament by myself. If I need any help, I'll let you know.

BABE ZAHARIAS TO HER PARTNER, PEGGY KIRK BELL, IN A FOUR-BALL EVENT IN THE 1950S

Women Who Seek Equality With Men Lack Ambition.

BUMPER STICKER SPORTED ON HER CAR BY PATSY SHEEHAN

The LPGA needs a player that looks like Farrah Fawcett and plays like Jack Nicklaus. Instead, they've got players who look like Jack Nicklaus and play like Farrah Fawcett.

ANON., *GOLF DIGEST*, 1981

We do not presume to dictate but must observe that the postures and gestures requisite for a full swing are not particularly graceful when the player is clad in female dress.

LORD WELLWOOD, 1890

I'd probably be the fat lady in a circus right now if it hadn't been for golf. It kept me on the course and out of the refrigerator.

KATHY WHITWORTH, TOP AMERICAN LPGA PROFESSIONAL

If you do that once more I shall slap your face.

THE REACTION TO GOLF JOURNALIST LEWINE MAIR, AFTER SHE HOLED PUTT AFTER PUTT IN A MATCH AGAINST AN UNNAMED OPPONENT

If [Laura Davies] used a driver off the tee and kept it in the fairway, the rest of us would be playing for second most of the time.

NANCY LOPEZ

Maybe their presence has contributed to the extraordinarily high standard of golf we have seen this week. A more likely explanation for the quality golf is that seeing their wives on the course, the golfers relax, knowing their credit cards are safe.

DAVID WALSH, WRITING IN *THE SUNDAY TIMES*, ABOUT THE ROLE OF THE PLAYERS' WIVES AT THE 1999 RYDER CUP AT BROOKLINE

Now the honeymoon can really start!

JACKIE CROWE, AFTER SPENDING HER HONEYMOON PLAYING IN THE MCDONALDS LPGA CHAMPIONSHIP IN 1998. SHE WAS MARRIED THE PREVIOUS SATURDAY AND, PERHAPS UNDERSTANDABLY, SHE MISSED THE CUT

If I didn't have these I'd hit it twenty yards further.

BABE ZAHARIAS, ON HER BREASTS

I've always had a wife – golf. No man should have more than one.

FRED MCLEOD, 1908 US OPEN WINNER, ON WHY HE NEVER MARRIED

It was the best round of golf I'd ever seen played. There were no fireworks produced, only faultless golf. Vardon, Duncan and Bobby Jones, when I played them, were wont to produce fireworks from time to time ... but this round of Miss Wethered's was above that class.

ROBERT HARRIS, 1925 BRITISH AMATEUR CHAMPION, DESCRIBING A ROUND OF 72 MADE BY JOYCE WETHERED AT ROYAL NORTH DEVON

Some people say the suffragettes have acted very unwisely in destroying golf greens because this has made golfers very angry, yet what is there to fear from their anger? What have [male] golfers ever done for the Suffragette Cause, and what will they ever do if they are left in peace to play their game?

THE SUFFRAGETTE MAGAZINE, COMMENTING ON RECENT ATTACKS ON GOLF GREENS IN THE HOME COUNTIES OF ENGLAND, FEBRUARY 1913

The rumour that the Suffragettes were going to turn their wicked intentions to our golf courses, has unfortunately proved only too true, and during the past month they have managed to seriously injure some of the finest greens in the Metropolis. One can only hope ... that the wretched women will have grown tired of despoiling golf courses, and have decided to turn their attention to other methods of outrage.

HAROLD HILTON, EDITOR, GOLF MONTHLY, 1913

Now I don't dare throw a club!

JOANNE CARNER, AFTER WINNING THE BOB JONES AWARD FOR SPORTSMANSHIP, 1981

During the practice rounds, onlookers appeared to be alarmed at the professionals' generally scruffy appearance. It was even rumoured that one of the competitors had spent the night in the local prison on a charge of drunkenness. With the possibility that women might be watching, it was decided by the committee that a suit of clothing would be given to every competitor to spare unnecessary blushes.

A. J. DALCONEN, ON THE REASON WHY EACH COMPETITOR IN THE FIRST BRITISH OPEN IN 1860 WAS DRESSED IN THE EARL OF EGLINGTON'S GREEN TARTAN

....

Excuse me, madam, would you mind either standing back or closing your mouth – I've lost four balls already.

TED RAY, BRITISH COMIC, TO A SPECTATOR AT A CHARITY MATCH IN SCOTLAND, 1952

....

What a foolish thing for her to do. Now she'll have to play all her drives off the back tees.

BING CROSBY, ON HEARING OF A POSSIBLE SEX-CHANGE OPERATION FOR A WOMAN GOLFER

There's a full moon, and I'll tell you I've been affected. I'm pulling energy from all over the world. Friends from all over, from Tokyo, California, everywhere, are pulling for me. And I'm pulling in the vibes.

MUFFIN SPENCER-DEVLIN, THE SPORTING NEWS, 1982

I was stupid. I learned a lesson. When you have a fight with the club, the club always wins.

PATTI HAYES, US LPGA PROFESSIONAL, WHO INJURED HER FOOT AFTER ATTEMPTING TO KICK HER CLUB THE SAME DISTANCE AS HER GOLF BALL IN THE SAMARITAN TURQUOISE CLASSIC, 1984

No, I got my period.

DONNA CAPONI, ASKED WHETHER OR NOT SHE HAD
CHOKED DURING THE FINAL STAGES OF A TOURNAMENT,
1969

I don't have any particular hang-ups about superstitions. I did
try them all, but they didn't work.

KATHY WHITWORTH, AFTER RECORDING HER 86TH LPGA
TOUR WIN IN 1984

In Japan, any player who scores a hole-in-one while leading the
tournament always loses. It's a proven jinx.

AYAKO OKAMOTO, US LPGA PROFESSIONAL

I've quit worrying about poor shots. I just tell myself, 'Relax,
Bozo. If you can't have fun, you shouldn't be out there.'

PATTY SHEEHAN, LEGENDARY AMERICAN PRO

I realize that's why we play golf, to hit the ball into the hole. But
it is a strange feeling when you hit the shot and it actually goes
in!

HOLLIS STACY, AFTER HOLING AN APPROACH SHOT FROM
123 YARDS DURING THE US WOMEN'S OPEN, 1984

The best result as a whole that she [the woman golfer] can hope
to attain is, after all, to play as good a comparative game of golf
as a man. She can learn to win without vain boasting, and lose
with a good grace, and take upon herself the complexion of
those who play the game for the actual enduring love of it.

LILIAN BROOKE, WRITING IN THE *NEW YORK TIMES*, 1900

Putting – the Game within a Game

Putting is like wisdom. Partly a natural gift and partly the accumulation of experience.

ARNOLD PALMER

I once shot a wild, charging elephant in Africa and it kept coming at me until dropping to the ground at my feet. I wasn't a bit scared. It takes a four-foot putt to scare me to death.

SAM SNEAD, ON THE PRESSURES OF GOLF

Drive for show, putt for dough.

A COMMON GOLF SAYING

Reading a green is like reading the small type in a contract. If you don't read it with painstaking care, you are likely to be in trouble.

CLAUDE HAMILTON, AMERICAN GOLF COACH

There is one problem with this game as far as I'm concerned: the hole will never come to the ball.

FRED DALY, IRISH-BORN WINNER OF THE BRITISH OPEN CHAMPIONSHIP IN 1947, WHO WAS RENOWNED FOR HIS WRISTY PUTTING STROKE

There's just no way to make the hole look bigger.

TOMMY ARMOUR

The game would be nothing without this troublesome business round the hole.

JOYCE WETHERED, TOP BRITISH WOMAN GOLFER OF THE 1920s

The way I putted, I must've been reading the greens in Spanish and putting them in English.

HOMERO BLANCAS

When you get up there in years, the fairways get longer and the holes get smaller.

BOBBY LOCKE, SOUTH AFRICAN PROFESSIONAL KNOWN FOR HIS PUTTING

The trouble with golf is you're only as good as your last putt.

DOUG SANDERS

To putt well ought to be the aim of every beginner; and, as he can practise it on any greensward, it is his own fault if he does not succeed.

ANON., THE GAME OF GOLF, c.1870

Putting affects the nerves more than anything. I would actually get nauseated over three-footers, and there were tournaments when I couldn't keep a meal down for four days.

BYRON NELSON

Half of golf is fun; the other half is putting.

PETER DOBEREINER

You can always recover from a bad drive, but there's no recovering from a bad putt. It's missing those six-inchers that causes us to break up our sticks.

JIMMY DEMARET

There are no points for style when it comes to putting. It's getting the ball in the cup that counts.

BRIAN SWARBRICK, AMERICAN AUTHOR

Never break your putter and your driver in the same round or you're dead.

TOMMY BOLT

There's no need to tell one who has played a great deal of championship golf that it's the short game that decides the contests.

TOMMY ARMOUR

....

Gimme: an agreement between two losers who can't putt.

JIM BISHOP

....

A good player who is a great putter is a match for any golfer. A great hitter who cannot putt is a match for no one.

Ben Sayers, old-time Scottish professional

Short putts are missed because it is not physically possible to make the little ball travel over uncertain ground for three or four feet with any degree of regularity.

Walter Hagen

Long putts travel on the wings of chance.

Bernard Darwin

Prayer never seems to work for me on the golf course. I think this has something to do with my being a terrible putter.

Rev. Billy Graham

[Walter] Hagen said that no one remembers who finished second. But they still ask me if I ever think about that putt I missed to win the 1970 [British] Open at St Andrews. I tell them that it sometimes doesn't cross my mind for a full five minutes.

Doug Sanders, who ended up losing a play-off to the eventual winner, Jack Nicklaus

The approach putt is an all-important shot – finishing near the hole it spares the player all the holing-out anxieties and jerky snatches.

Robert Harris, *Sixty Years of Golf*, 1953

Putting from that distance [ninety feet] is a little like trying to touch a girl sitting on the far side of a couch. You can reach her, but you're not likely to accomplish much.

CHARLES PRICE, AMERICAN GOLF COLUMNIST AND AUTHOR

When our putting is sour ... then we are in honest, interminable, miserable trouble.

ARNOLD PALMER, ON HIS PUTTING IN THE 1970S

Hitting a golf ball and putting have nothing in common. They're two different games. You work all your life to perfect a repeating swing that will get you to the greens, and then you have to try to do something that is totally unrelated. There shouldn't be any cups, just flagsticks. And then the man who hit the most fairways and greens and got closest to the pins would be the tournament winner.

BEN HOGAN

The yips are that ghastly time when, with the first movement of the putter, the golfer blacks out, loses sight of the ball and hasn't the remotest idea of what to do with the putter or, occasionally, that he is holding a putter at all.

TOMMY ARMOUR

A grand player up to the green, and a very bad player when he got there. But then, Vardon gave himself less putting to do than any other man.

BERNARD DARWIN, BRITISH WRITER

The best putters have almost invariably been slow movers. Walter Hagen took five minutes to reach for and lift a salt shaker, 45 minutes to shave. He just never rushed into anything.

GEORGE LOW, *THE MASTER OF PUTTING*, 1983

My putting was atrocious. I changed grips, stance, you name it. I tried everything but standing on my head.

ARNOLD PALMER, ON HIS PUTTING PROBLEMS DURING THE 1968 US OPEN AT OAKHILL

That's a bagful of indecisions.

JACKIE BURKE, ON HEARING THAT ARNOLD PALMER'S CADDIE CARRIED EIGHT PUTTERS IN HIS BAG DURING A PRACTICE ROUND

It's that you lose nerves, not nerve. You can shoot lions in the dark and yet you can quiver like a leaf and fall flat over a two-foot putt.

JOHNNY FARRELL, AMERICAN PROFESSIONAL

....

This is a course where good putters worry about their second putt before they hit the first one.

LEW WORSHAM, CLUB PROFESSIONAL AT OAKMONT

....

Would you like to know how to sink those putts? Just hit the ball closer to the hole.

VALERIE HOGAN, OFFERING SOME ADVICE TO HUSBAND BEN DURING THE LOS ANGELES OPEN, 1937

My godfathers!

And my godmothers!

I have missed that putt again!

HENRY LEACH, *THE SPIRIT OF THE LINKS*, 1907

Do not get into the habit of pointing out the peculiarly salient blade of grass which you imagine to have been the cause of your failing to hole your putt. You may sometimes find your adversary who has successfully holed his, irritatingly short-sighted on these occasions. Moreover, the opinion of a man who has just missed his putt, about the state of the green, is usually accepted with some reserve.

HORACE HUTCHINSON, *HINTS ON GOLF*, 1896

Throw me that ball ... I thought so ... The bugger isn't round.

ARTHUR LEES, CLUB PROFESSIONAL AT SUNNINGDALE AND RENOWNED PUTTER, AFTER MISSING A 30-FOOT PUTT, 1948

I feel sorry for Casper. He can't putt a lick. He missed three 30-footers out there today.

GARY PLAYER, ON RIVAL BILLY CASPER, DURING THE 1964 US OPEN AT CONGRESSIONAL

The man who can putt is a match for anyone.

WILLIAM PARK JR, SCOTTISH PROFESSIONAL, CLUB-MAKER, AUTHOR AND TWICE BRITISH OPEN CHAMPION

I get confused. Sometimes when I look at a putt from one side, then go round the other side, I see another line!

IAN WOOSNAM, ON HIS OCCASIONAL PUTTING PROBLEMS

Hell, I'd putt sitting up in a coffin if I thought I could hole e something.

GARDNER DICKINSON, AMERICAN PROFESSIONAL KNOWN FOR HIS UNUSUAL PUTTING METHODS

When I saw that four-inch putt for a par at 18. I have a good percentage at handling four-inch putts.

HAL SUTTON, WINNER OF THE 1983 PGA CHAMPIONSHIP, ANSWERING THE QUESTION, 'WHEN DID YOU THINK YOU HAD WON THE CHAMPIONSHIP?'

Most of us will banish the offending club to the attic or at least a darkened room until it has learned its lesson, or until you feel more disposed to giving it a last chance. Such a putter is a Par One model I obtained in a fenland pro shop 30 years ago in exchange for a £25 voucher I'd won in a competition. It's heavy, heel-toe weighted and I can flick the ball up on the back of the flange and toss it in the air before catching it. I loved it until about a year ago, when I was given a couple of replacements, custom-fitted for me by generous manufacturers, who'd seen me three-putt too often for my putter to be totally blameless. My old putter was banished ... until Sunday morning ... I suddenly spotted its dull little brass head peeking out from behind the freezer. With its shortened 31-inch shaft and distinctive thick Tiger Shark grip, it felt as comfortable as ever but it looked so forlorn. It needed a make-over. Now, my good lady will tell you I can clean brass for England. It's one of the few household chores you can do without taking your eyes off golf or the World Cup on the telly, apart from shelling peas – and there's not much call for that these days. Within minutes with a splash of Brasso and a soft cloth, my old putter was shining like a new £2 coin. Call me an old romantic if you like, but that putter behaved impeccably and I proceeded to take only 30 putts in 18 holes – and for me that's outrageously good.

The moral of this story is to look after your putter and it will look after you. Treat it with tender loving care and it will respond by delivering a feel-good factor that only comes when the ball starts rolling into the hole with thrilling monotony.

BOB WARTERS, IN HIS EDITORIAL FOR *GOLF WEEKLY*, 1999

Do not allow yourself to be annoyed because your opponent insists on making elaborate study of all his putts.

HORACE HUTCHINSON, 1890

Bad putting is due more to the effect the green has upon the player than it has upon the action of the ball.

BOBBY JONES

Once upon a time there was a rabbit which played a very remarkable practical joke upon some of us at Westward Ho! With great discrimination it refrained from any onset upon the turf in the neighbourhood of the hole which might have given warning of its presence, but made use of the hole itself as an entry providentially constructed, and dug down from the bottom of the hole nobody ever discovered how far. Of course, the result was that as party after party came to the hole they putted out but were altogether unable to retrieve the ball which had gone down into the very bowels of the earth.

HORACE HUTCHINSON, 'MEMORIES OF WESTWARD HO!', *THE MIDLAND GOLFER*, 1914

Putting is the department of golf which ... lends itself to experimentation and the exploitation of pet theories.

HARRY VARDON, SIX TIMES BRITISH OPEN CHAMPION, WHO SUFFERED DREADFULLY FROM THE 'YIPS' IN THE LATER YEARS OF HIS CAREER

Even when times were good, I realized that my earning power as a golf professional depended on too many ifs and putts.

GENE SARAZEN

Miss 'em quick!

MACDONALD SMITH, TOP TOURNAMENT PROFESSIONAL OF THE 1930s

Mr Edmunds had told me – it was the only direct advice I remember he ever gave me – that no good golfer ever took more than two putts. This was Law, the greens were small, and I seldom did.

ARTHUR RAINSFORD, BRITISH WRITER, 1962

Remember that Walter Hagen and other great golfers miss putts, even as you and I, but they don't miss 'em in advance.

CHARLES FLETCHER, AMERICAN HUMORIST, ON THE PROBLEMS WITH NEGATIVE THOUGHTS ON THE GREEN

We played 36 holes and Taylor never got a hole in front of me from start to finish, and I never was more than one up. It was neck and neck all the way. The strain was 'gey bad'. There was one hole in the last round where he had a chance. The ground was hard and keen and a little wind was blowing. Both our balls

> Talking turkey to a businessman, you must look squarely at him during the entire conversation. It's the same with putting. When you're talking turkey on the green, the face of your putter must look squarely at the hole.
> GENE SARAZEN

lay on the green, not more than a foot from the hole and perhaps only ten inches. I said, 'A half?' to Taylor. 'No, Andrew,' he said. 'You play.' His ball was about an inch in front of mine. I said, 'Lift your ball, then.' I played and missed. The ball struck the side of the hole and dribbled a yard past on the keen green. It was like putting on a window. Taylor must, at that moment, have felt pleased that he decided to play instead of halving the hole. But holes are never lost or won till the ball is out of sight.

It was absurd to think that Taylor would miss a ten-inch putt.

ANDREW KIRKALDY, DESCRIBING A MATCH AGAINST THE LEGENDARY PUTTER, J. H. TAYLOR, AT ST ANDREWS IN 1902

A forward press on the green ... is one infallible characteristic of the very bad putter.

HENRY LONGHURST

One often finds that a good billiard player makes a good golfer, because he has such a full appreciation of the different effects upon a little ball according to the precise manner in which it is struck. And the superior training of his eye stands him in very good stead on the putting greens.

JAMES BRAID, *HOW TO PLAY GOLF*, 1901

A putt of a club's length which is to determine not merely the hole but the match will try the calmness even of an experienced performer, and many there are who have played golf all their lives whose pulse beats quicker when they have to play the stroke. No slave ever scanned the expression of a tyrannical master with half the miserable anxiety with which the performer surveys the ground over which the hole is to be approached. He looks at the hole from the ball, and he looks at the ball from the hole. No blade of grass, no scarcely perceptible inclination of the surface, escapes his critical inspection. He puts off the decisive moment as long, and perhaps longer, than he decently can. If he be a man who dreads responsibility, he asks the advice of his caddie, of his partner, and of his partner's caddie, so that the particular method in which he proposes to approach the hole represents not so much his own individual policy as the policy of a Cabinet. At last the stroke is made, and immediately all tongues are loosened. The slowly advancing ball is addressed in tones of menace or entreaty by the surrounding players. It is requested to go on or stop; to turn this way or that, as the respective interests of each party require. Nor is there anything more entertaining than seeing half a dozen faces bending over this little bit of moving gutta-percha which so remorselessly obeys the laws of dynamics. And pouring out on it threatenings and supplications not to be surpassed in apparent fervour by the devotions of any fetish worshippers in existence.

A. J. BALFOUR, FORMER BRITISH PRIME MINISTER, ON THE MENTAL ANGUISH INVOLVED IN HOLING A THREE-FOOT PUTT, GOLF, 1890

Putting is really a game within a game.

TOM WATSON, GOLF WORLD

Anybody can drive, but it takes a golfer to putt.

ANDREW KIRKALDY, OLD-TIME SCOTTISH PROFESSIONAL, 1891

My experience shows conclusively that the really good putter is largely born, not made and is inherently endowed with a good eye and tactile delicacy of grip which are denied the ordinary run of mortals.

WALTER TRAVIS, 1900 AMERICAN AMATEUR CHAMPION

The newspapers wrote that I personally lost the Ryder Cup. Sure I missed a short putt on the 17th to win, but so did many others that day. But they put me on the front pages. It was amazing. I missed a little putt and I became famous.

COSTANTINO ROCCA, ON THE CRITICISM HE FACED AFTER EUROPE LOST THE 1993 RYDER CUP AT THE BELFRY

He told me just to keep the ball low.

CHI CHI RODRIGUEZ, ON SOME HELPFUL PUTTING ADVICE FROM HIS CADDIE, GOLF MONTHLY

On Sunday, I swept my garage and practised ten-footers on the concrete.
PAUL STANKOWSKI, ON THE REASON HE SHOT A FIRST-
ROUND 68 IN THE 1997 US MASTERS AT AUGUSTA

My driving's really wonderful,
My iron play's superb,
My mashie play is reasonable,
But my putting is absurd.
'GOLFER'S LAMENT', c.1899

I think it is slightly straight, Mr Faulkner.
MAX FAULKNER, 1951 BRITISH OPEN CHAMPION AND
FORMER RYDER CUP PLAYER, ON HOW HE ONCE RECEIVED
THE LINE FROM HIS CADDIE

Putt with your ears is a good motto. Wait until you can hear the
ball fall into the tin. Then don't look at the hole. You will get
far more satisfaction by looking at the face of your opponent.
JACK WHITE, 1904 BRITISH OPEN CHAMPION

Sure I felt nervous [over that last putt]. Back in those days the
short putts were a lot easier than they are today.
TOM WATSON, ON HIS THREE-FOOT PUTT TO WIN THE
1977 BRITISH OPEN AT TURNBERRY

I had a long putt for an eleven.

CLAYTON HEAFNER, ON WHY HE TOOK A TWELVE ON ONE
PARTICULAR HOLE

Not only are three-putt greens probable, at times they are an achievement.

CHARLEY PRIDE, AMERICAN COUNTRY AND WESTERN
SINGER, ON HIS PUTTING PROBLEMS IN THE 1970s

Everyone wants to be known as a great striker of the ball for some reason. Nobody wants to be called a lucky, one-putting s.o.b.

GARY PLAYER

Celebrity Golf

Give me golf clubs, the fresh air and a beautiful partner and you can keep my golf clubs and the fresh air.

JACK BENNY, AMERICAN COMIC

Golf has taught me there is a connection between pleasure and pain. 'Golf' spelled backwards is 'flog'.

PHYLLIS DILLER, HOLLYWOOD STAR

I like to play in the low 70s. If it gets any hotter than that I'll stay in the bar!

BOB HOPE

I think golf is good for boxing, but the reverse is far from being the case.

MAX BAER, FORMER WORLD HEAVYWEIGHT CHAMPION

One minute it's fear and loathing, but hit a couple of good shots and you're on top of the world. I've gone crazy over this game.

JACK NICHOLSON

Grass? Give me a bucket of balls and a sand wedge. Sure I like grass.

> IVAN LENDL, TENNIS PROFESSIONAL, WHO WON EIGHT
> GRAND SLAM TOURNAMENTS, BUT NOT ONE ON GRASS

If you think it's hard to meet new people, try picking up the wrong golf ball.

> JACK LEMMON

Obviously she has seen you tee off before and knows that the safest place to be when you play is right down the middle.

> JACKIE GLEASON, TO WRITER MILTON GROSS, AFTER
> SPOTTING A DEER GRAZING IN THE FAIRWAY

I was a little nervous, but Hale gave me such great reassurance that I relaxed and eliminated a lot of the carnage.

> SEAN CONNERY, ON THE HELP HE RECEIVED FROM FORMER
> US OPEN CHAMPION HALE IRWIN BEFORE PLAYING IN A
> PRO-AM EVENT AT LA QUINTA, CALIFORNIA

My handicap is that I am a one-eyed Negro.

> SAMMY DAVIS JR

I've got one hole that's a par-23 and a couple of times I've come mighty close to birdieing that sucker.

> WILLIE NELSON, COUNTRY AND WESTERN STAR, WHO BUILT
> HIS OWN COURSE ON HIS RANCH AT AUSTIN, TEXAS

I have no butt. You need a butt if you're going to hit a golf ball.

DENNIS QUAID

On one hole I'm like Arnold Palmer, and on the next like Lilli Palmer.

SEAN CONNERY

I'd give up golf if I didn't have so many sweaters.

BOB HOPE

It was a great honour to be inducted into the Hall of Fame. I didn't know they had a caddie division.

BOB HOPE

I can tell right away if a guy is a winner or a loser just by the way he conducts himself on the course.

DONALD TRUMP, US MULTI-MILLIONAIRE BUSINESSMAN

If you drink, don't drive. Don't even putt.

DEAN MARTIN

Jack Lemmon has been in more bunkers than Eva Braun.

PHIL HARRIS, AMERICAN COMIC

You've heard of Arnie's Army. Well, those are Dean's Drunks.

DEAN MARTIN

My best score ever is 103. But then again I've only been playing for 13 years.

ALEX KARRAS, AMERICAN PRO FOOTBALL LEGEND

Davis Love III turned me on to golf when we were at North Carolina by showing me it wasn't a sissy game.

MICHAEL JORDAN, US BASKETBALL STAR

He who has the fastest golf cart never has a bad lie.

MICKEY MANTLE, US BASEBALL STAR

Al Capone was not a particularly able golfer, but he played honestly and with enjoyment.

NEW YORKER, 1937

Be funny on a golf course? Do I kid my best friend's mother about her heart condition?

PHIL SILVERS, THE GREAT 'SGT BILKO' HIMSELF

I would rather play Hamlet on Broadway with no rehearsal than tee off at Pebble Beach on television.

JACK LEMMON

Every rock 'n' roll band I know, guys with long hair and tattoos, plays golf now.

ALICE COOPER, AMERICAN ROCK STAR AND KEEN GOLFER

I couldn't tell you exactly what I like about golf. Just when you think you've got it mastered it lets you know you haven't. I'm just crazy enough to do it.

CLINT EASTWOOD

The hardest shot is a mashie at ninety yards from the green, where the ball has to be played against an oak tree, bounces back into a sand trap, hits a stone, bounces on the green and then rolls into the cup. That shot is so difficult I have only made it once.

ZEPPO MARX

....

If that's true, I'm the first dead man to make six double bogeys.

VICTOR MATURE, AMERICAN FILM STAR, ON THE GOLF
COURSE WHEN HIS DEATH WAS REPORTED ON THE RADIO,
1982

....

Golfers are more like celebrities now. Tiger Woods is a superstar. But, oh, by the way, he's also a golfer. This is one place you can't take pictures of celebrities. It's a tough rule, but out here one stroke can cost a guy a lot of money or even an exemption for next year. It used to be that you had only golf fans at golf tournaments. But now there are more and more people who don't know golf. They think they can yell at golfers the way they yell at basketball players. Today it's become accepted that you can yell at a player. It started with that 'You da man' stuff. I'm not just standing up for myself but for the etiquette of the game.

DAVIS LOVE III, ON AMATEUR PHOTOGRAPHERS AT GOLF
TOURNAMENTS

I think I've got the idea now.

HOAGY CARMICHAEL, LEGENDARY SONGWRITER, AFTER AN
ACE AT PEBBLE BEACH

She just let out the biggest yell you have ever heard. It scared the daylights out of me. She just freaked out!

> MARK O'MEARA, EXPLAINING WHAT HAPPENED ON A
> FAMILY TRIP TO A BURGER BAR IN ORLANDO WHEN HE AND
> HIS GOOD FRIEND TIGER WOODS WERE RECOGNIZED BY ONE
> OF THE EMPLOYEES

I find it to be the hole-in-one.

> GROUCHO MARX, ON THE MOST DIFFICULT SHOT HE FACED
> DURING A ROUND OF GOLF

I enjoy the tournament. The atmosphere is great. But the main thing will be seeing if we can get Jack through the cut.

> NICK FALDO, ON BEING PAIRED WITH JACK LEMMON IN THE
> 1998 AT&T PEBBLE BEACH PRO-AM – AN EVENT IN
> WHICH THE ACTOR HAS NEVER PROGRESSED BEYOND THE
> HALF-WAY STAGE

It reminded me of a similar incident involving Nigel Mansell about four years ago. I'd been visiting him at his home in America and we were on a nearby golf course when he also suddenly changed direction unexpectedly in a golf cart. Obviously he's used to far greater speeds and I flew out of that cart like a projected missile – luckily I wasn't hurt at all!

> MARK McNULTY, EUROPEAN TOUR PROFESSIONAL, ON THE
> HAZARDS OF PLAYING GOLF WITH A FORMER WORLD
> CHAMPION FORMULA 1 DRIVER, 1998

My boomerang drive is the talk of all the golf clubs where I play. I drive well out to the left and it's a joy to see the ball coming back into the centre of the fairway. Of course I occasionally hit a straight one and that doesn't half mess me up. But I'm very good at keeping the score. With members of the Vaudeville Golfing Society you need to be! I played a fellow last week – a liar if ever there was one – and I knew he was cheating about the number of strokes he had taken. He said he'd won the hole! Anyway I went carefully through the shots we had taken, and he had to agree that we had halved in 23.

ARTHUR ASKEY, BRITISH COMIC

In front of a big gallery, I was duly announced and subsequently missed the ball on the tee shot. Everyone thought I was being funny since I am known somewhat as a bit of a lad. The second attempt, however, almost killed some of the gallery. There was no more laughter then, as they realized that I was a very nervous actor, trying to look like a golfer.

LESLIE PHILLIPS, BRITISH COMIC ACTOR, ON PLAYING IN HIS FIRST CELEBRITY PRO-AM

I'm afraid the world has not seen a more completely non-golf person than myself. The game is an absolutely closed book to me and I would not even know which end to swing a caddie.

DENIS NORDEN, BRITISH COMEDY WRITER AND TELEVISION PRESENTER

My old friend Jack Benny has only had one ball all his golfing life. And now he has lost it. The string came off!

BOB HOPE

Bing Crosby and I play a lot of golf together and I have a small course at my place where we often play for side stakes. The only trouble is that when I win, I always have to engage an attorney before I can draw the money.

BOB HOPE

[Bob] Hope invented the nonbody turn, the interlocking grip on a money clip, the fast backswing and a good short game – off the tee!

BING CROSBY

How could a guy who won the West, recaptured Bataan and won the battle of Iwo Jima let himself be defeated by a little hole in the ground?

JAMES E. GRANT, AMERICAN SCREENWRITER, ON JOHN WAYNE AND HIS STATED INTENTION TO GIVE UP GOLF

At a certain stage in one's life one must either give up serious golf altogether, or turn professional. I made my decision at the age of eight and gave away my only club – a driver, which I used for every shot – and have felt better ever since.

MICHAEL BENTINE

You know you're not going to wind up with anything but grief but you just can't resist the impulse.

JACKIE GLEASON, COMPARING GOLF WITH DATING WOMEN

The fun you get from golf is in direct ratio to the effort you don't put into it.

BOB ALLEN, AMERICAN COMEDIAN

The Mental Side of Golf

After you get the basics down, it's all mental.

KEN VENTURI

Few games show the character of a person more than does that of golf.

W. H. G. KINGSTON, *ERNEST BRACEBRIDGE, OR SCHOOLBOY DAYS*, 1860

Let's face it, 95 per cent of this game is mental. If a guy plays lousy golf he doesn't need a pro, he needs a shrink.

TOM MURPHY, US PGA PROFESSIONAL

In the midst of that wilderness I chanced upon a somewhat chubby gentleman engaged in the pursuit of a small white ball, which, when he came within striking distance, he beat savagely with weapons of wood and iron. That, sir, was my first sight of you, and my earliest acquaintance with the game of golf. I remember scanning the horizon for your keeper.

CHARLES E. VAN LOAN, 1918

I feel calm in calm colours. I don't want people to watch the way I dress. I want people to watch the way I play.

SEVE BALLESTEROS, *GOLF MONTHLY*, 1979

Golf is a funny game. It's done much for health, and at the same time has ruined people by robbing them of their peace of mind. Look at me, I'm the healthiest idiot in the world.

BOB HOPE

....

[They're] parasites. Everything that needs to be said about the mental side of golf could be written on a single sheet of paper.

MARK JAMES, FORMER RYDER CUP CAPTAIN, ON THE RISE OF GOLF PSYCHOLOGISTS

....

Human nature is so funny, it is a thousand pities that neither Aristotle nor Shakespeare was a golfer. There is no game that strips the soul so naked.

HORACE HUTCHINSON, 1901

I always thought with my distance, Majors would be the easiest tournaments for me to win. [But] I never realized how important putting was, and how mentally hard it was. I have lost tournaments by trying too hard on the greens.

DAVIS LOVE III

It's a shame, but he'll never make a golfer — too much temper.

ALEX SMITH, SCOTTISH PROFESSIONAL, ON BOBBY JONES, 1915

You must expect anything in golf. A stranger comes through, he's keen for a game, he seems affable enough, and on the eighth fairway he turns out to be an idiot.

ALISTAIR COOKE, 1957

It can happen pretty quickly and is very frightening for a golfer who has won a Major title. All of a sudden it's not there in the morning. You just reach the first tee and get butterflies just wondering whether you are going to get through without having a disaster. Then you knock it out-of-bounds or something and the tournament is over for you after just a few holes. You go to the next tournament and there it is again. You reach the stage when you finally do shoot a good round that you start to question whether it was good golf or pure luck. It takes a very strong mind to shut out such thoughts.

SANDY LYLE, ON THE PRO GOLFER'S NIGHTMARE — A LONG-TERM SLUMP IN FORM — IN *THE ROUND OF MY LIFE*, 1998

How would you like to meet the top 143 people at what you do each week in order to survive?

BRUCE CRAMPTON, US TOUR PROFESSIONAL

Ladies and Gentlemen — may I present the finest golfers in the world.

US RYDER CUP CAPTAIN, BEN HOGAN, ATTEMPTING TO GAIN THE MENTAL EDGE AT THE OPENING CEREMONY TO THE 1967 MATCH AT HOUSTON, TEXAS

I'm not an intellectual person. I don't get headaches from concentration. I get them from double bogeys.

TOM WEISKOPF, 1973 BRITISH OPEN CHAMPION

They were real golfers, for real golf is a thing of the spirit, not of mere mechanical excellence of stroke.

P. G. WODEHOUSE, 'A WOMAN IS ONLY A WOMAN', 1919

I don't think I had enough sense to know what pressure was.

GENE SARAZEN

Golf, perhaps through its very slowness, can reach the most extraordinary heights of tenseness and drama.

HENRY LONGHURST, 'A HARD CASE FROM TEXAS', 1957

There's more tension in golf than in boxing because golfers bring it on themselves. It's silly really because it's not as if the golf ball is going to jump up and belt you on the whiskers, is it?

HENRY COOPER, BRITISH HEAVYWEIGHT BOXING CHAMPION

Serenity is knowing that your worst shot is still going to be pretty good.

JOHNNY MILLER

Unlike that other Scottish game of whisky drinking, excess in golf is not injurious to the health.

SIR WALTER SIMPSON

The average player would rather play than watch. Those who don't play can't possibly appreciate the subtleties of the game. Trying to get their attention with golf is like selling Shakespeare in the neighbourhood saloon.

BOB TOSKI

In other games you get another chance. In baseball you get three cracks at it; in tennis you lose only one point. But in golf the loss of one shot has been responsible for the loss of heart.

TOMMY ARMOUR, 1931 BRITISH OPEN WINNER

The least thing upset him on the links. He missed short putts because of the uproar of the butterflies in the adjoining meadows.

P. G. WODEHOUSE

A lot of guys who have never choked have never been in the position to do so.

TOM WATSON

The game was easy for me as a kid, and I had to play a while to find out how hard it is.

RAYMOND FLOYD

I wouldn't say I'm extra intelligent.

COLIN MONTGOMERIE, DISCUSSING HIS DEGREE IN LAW

I'm about five inches from being an outstanding golfer. That's the distance my left ear is from my right.

BEN CRENSHAW

I don't care what anybody says. The first tournament is not the hardest one to win. It's always the second one.

JOHN DALY

It is ... in the mind and not the body that the cause of every golfing ailment is to be sought, and this being so, it is the mind which requires treatment and not the body, as is the customary procedure.

MAJOR G. F. MAPPIN, *THE GOLFING YOU*, 1948

When I'm in this state, everything is pure, vividly clear. I'm in a cocoon of concentration.

TONY JACKLIN, TALKING AFTER HIS 1970 US OPEN VICTORY AT HAZELTINE

Staying in the present is the key to any golfer's game. Once you start thinking about a shot you just messed up or what you have to do on the next nine to catch somebody, you're lost.

PAUL AZINGER

It's too far away to spend half an hour on the phone talking to him.

SANDY LYLE, TALKING ABOUT HIS AUSTRALIAN-BASED GOLF PSYCHOLOGIST

The inferior player should never, never in any way behave differently, let alone apologize, because he is inferior. In the days when I was genuinely young and had muscles like whipcord I used to drive nearly 210 yards on the downhill hole at Redhill. My father's best was 140 yards. As soon as he had struck one of these hundred-and-forty-yarders, he would stand stock still gazing after the ball till it had stopped and then pace the distance, counting out loud, and ending in a crescendo 'a hundred and thirty-eight, thirty-nine, FORTY'.

STEPHEN POTTER, *THE COMPLETE GOLF GAMESMANSHIP*,
1968

Golf is a spiritual game. It's like Zen; you have to let your mind take over.

AMY ALCOTT, FORMER AMERICAN LPGA TOUR PLAYER

Golf cannot be played in anger, or in any mood of emotional excess. Half the golf balls struck by amateurs are hit if not in rage surely in bewilderment, or gloom, or in cynicism, or even hysterically — all of those emotional excesses must be contained by the professional. Which is why balance is one of the essential ingredients of golf. Professionals invariably trudge phlegmatically around the course — whatever emotions are seething within — with the grim yet placid and bored look of cowpokes, slack-bodied in their saddles, who have been tending the same herd for two months.

GEORGE PLIMPTON, BRITISH JOURNALIST AND AUTHOR

I guess there is nothing that will get your mind off everything like golf. I have never been depressed enough to take up the game, but they say you get so sore at yourself you forget to hate your enemies.

WILL ROGERS, AMERICAN POLITICAL SATIRIST

I'd play every day if I could. It's cheaper than a shrink and there are no telephones on my golf cart.

BRENT MUSBERGER, TOP US SPORTS PRESENTER

Golf acts as a corrective against sinful pride. I attribute the insane arrogance of the later Roman emperors almost entirely to the fact that, never having played golf, they never knew that strange chastening humility which is engendered by a topped chip shot.

P. G. WODEHOUSE, *WODEHOUSE ON GOLF*, 1973

You have to take this game through so many labyrinths of the mind, past all the traps – like, will my masculinity be threatened if I hit the ball well and still shoot 72?

MAC O'GRADY, FORMER US TOUR PRO TURNED GOLF TEACHER

Good golfing temperament falls somewhere between taking it with a grin or shrug and throwing a fit.

SAM SNEAD

The formula for par golf depends on three main factors – viz., Practice, Automatism and Reason (devoid of temperamental and other mental divergence), and the formula itself would be P+A+R=PAR.

THEODORE HYSLOP, SEARCHING FOR THE ALL-ELUSIVE SECRET OF HOW TO PLAY PAR GOLF, *MENTAL HANDICAPS IN GOLF*, 1927

I think it's harder to win now. Everything is more precise. Players use video cameras to analyse their swing. They are also more athletic. The mental and physical aspects are better. And the golf ball makes it hard for one person to win a lot. Today's ball doesn't curve the way it used to.

CHARLIE WARD, BRITISH RYDER CUP PROFESSIONAL OF THE 1950s

Excessive golfing dwarfs the intellect. Nor is this to be wondered at when we consider that the more fatuously vacant the mind is, the better for play. It has been observed that absolute idiots play the steadiest.

SIR WALTER SIMPSON, *THE ART OF GOLF*, 1887

We all know quite a bit about Jean Van de Velde and he's very good. The one thing we don't know, and he doesn't know until he's been there, is how he can cope with the situation now.

COLIN MONTGOMERIE, SPEAKING THE NIGHT BEFORE THE FINAL ROUND OF THE 1999 BRITISH OPEN AT CARNOUSTIE. LESS THAN 24 HOURS LATER, VAN DE VELDE STUMBLED TO A FINAL HOLE TRIPLE-BOGEY AFTER LEADING BY THREE SHOTS GOING UP THE LAST

The golfer has more enemies than any other athlete. He has 14 clubs in his bag, all of them different; 18 holes to play, all of them different, every week; and all around him are sand, trees, grass, water, wind, and 143 other players. In addition, the game is 50 per cent mental, so his biggest enemy is himself.

DAN JENKINS, TOP AMERICAN SPORTS JOURNALIST AND AUTHOR

I've had to handle things that, quite frankly, not too many 21-year-olds have to handle.

TIGER WOODS

Competitive golf is played mainly on a five-and-a-half-inch course, the space between your ears.

BOBBY JONES

Golf giveth and golf taketh away. But it taketh away a hell of a lot more than it giveth.

SIMON HOBDAY, FORMER EUROPEAN TOUR PROFESSIONAL

Neither your drive nor your approach nor your putt is determined by a psychic monitor flitting through your brain, nor by an unimaginable soul sitting in your glandula pinealis; they are determined by your nerves and muscles, by what you have been, by what you have learned, by what you have eaten and drunk. Never mind about psycho-physical parallelism. Keep muscle and nerve in good working order; be clean and honest; take lessons; learn; and be careful about what you eat and drink.

ANON.

The trouble with me is I think too much. I always said you have to be dumb to play good golf.

JOANNE CARNER

You don't know what pressure is until you play for five bucks with only two bucks in your pocket.

LEE TREVINO

These are the hazards of golf: the unpredictability of your own body chemistry, the rub of the green on the courses, the wind and the weather, the bee that lands on your ball or on the back of your neck while you are putting, the sudden noise while you are swinging, the whole problem of playing the game at high mental tension and low physical tension.

ARNOLD PALMER

Why do you keep putting yourself through this?

NICK FALDO, AFTER PULLING HIS DRIVE INTO TROUBLE DURING THE THIRD ROUND OF THE 1998 VOLVO MASTERS IN SPAIN

To the onlooker she is phlegmatic, cold, no nerves. Yet after a strenuous week of Championship golf, she is forced to rest and leave golf for a fortnight or more.

GLENNA COLLETT, LEGENDARY AMERICAN GOLFER, ON HER GREATEST RIVAL, JOYCE WETHERED, 1926

I know the feeling of standing on a tee with real fear in my heart, the match slipping away and the club feeling strange.

JOYCE WETHERED, FOUR TIMES BRITISH LADIES CHAMPION, ON THE STRAIN OF PERFORMING, 1933

I do a lot of humming out on the course. I tend to stick with one song ... I shot a 66 to 'Moon River'.

JACK NICKLAUS, ON HOW HE RELAXES DURING TOURNAMENT PLAY, 1978

A tolerable day, a tolerable green, a tolerable opponent, supply, or ought to supply, all that any reasonably constituted human being should require in the way of entertainment. With a fine sea view, and a clear course in front of him, the golfer should find no difficulty in dismissing all worries from his mind.

A. J. BALFOUR, GOLF, 1890

I think if you have a positive thought, you're more likely to make a positive golf swing.

VIJAY SINGH, ON HIS WAY TO WINNING THE 1998 UNITED STATES PGA CHAMPIONSHIP

Golf is an open exhibition of overweening ambition, courage deflated by stupidity, skill soured by a whiff of arrogance ... These humiliations are the essence of the game.

ALISTAIR COOKE

Golf is a game requiring an enormous amount of thought, and unless the player can always ascertain exactly what is the reason for his faults and what is the reason for his method of remedying them he will never make much progress. The more he thinks out the game for himself the better he will get on.

JAMES BRAID, HOW TO PLAY GOLF, 1901

Every golfer has a little monster in him, it's just that type of sport.

FUZZY ZOELLER

Not long ago two golfers, close friends, were playing over a California course. A dispute over scores led to the fatal shooting of one and the committing suicide by the other. Physicians agreed that the man who did the shooting temporarily was insane. Yet, just how much of a gap existed between the mental status of the golfer who did the shooting and the wrathful fury many otherwise sane golfers allow to lay hold of themselves?

FRANK C. TONE, *WARDING OFF THE BRAINSTORM*, 1928

There are things there are as unfathomable as they are fascinating to the masculine mind: metaphysics, golf and the feminine heart. The Germans, I believe, pretend to have solved some of the riddles of the first, and the French to have unravelled some of the intricacies of the second; will someone tell us wherein lies the extraordinary fascination of the last?

ARNOLD HAULTAIN, *THE MYSTERY OF GOLF*, 1910

The sages of the past averred that at least three parts of a golfer's difficulties were mental. It is now apparent that this was a reasonable assumption.

ROBERT HARRIS, *SIXTY YEARS OF GOLF*, 1953

One of the most interesting phenomena seen on a modern links is the Coué or self-hypnotic species; such gentlemen will stand for hours with their eyes glued on the ball, motionless, as does a cat watching the antics of its victim, then suddenly, as a spring released from tension, they burst into life and flog the ball in every possible direction except perhaps the right one.

H. MACNEILE DIXON, *GOLF AND HOW*, 1944

While, on the whole, playing through the green is the part of the game most trying to the temper, putting is that most trying to the nerves. There is always hope that a bad drive may be redeemed by a fine approach shot, or that a 'foozle' with the brassy may be balanced by some brilliant performance with the iron. But when the stage of putting-out has been reached, no further illusions are possible – no place for repentance remains. To succeed in such a case is to win the hole; to fail, is to lose it.

A. J. BALFOUR, ON THE MENTAL ANGUISH INVOLVED IN
HOLING A TRICKY PUTT, GOLF, 1890

When one has the misfortune to play against 'the man with a temper', the very greatest tact and knowledge of human nature are necessary, if one is to attempt to soothe his savage breast. 'Touch not the cat without the glove.' But the devastating and demoralizing effect of the golfing temper, on even the finest natures, is so terrible, that it is extremely dangerous to say anything, however apparently sympathetic, and the patient is much better left severely alone, until the paroxysm has passed.

J. H. TAYLOR, FIVE TIMES BRITISH OPEN CHAMPION

Golf is a game which brings out the peculiarities and idiosyncrasies of human nature. It permits no compromises, recognizes no weaknesses and punishes the foolhardy. Yet the apparent simplicity involved in hitting a small white ball from A to B lures all potential golfers into a false sense of security. Every instinct in the human psyche says the game looks easy, therefore it must be. That, for many of us, is where the trouble starts.

A. J. DALCONEN, *GOLF: THE HISTORY OF THE ROYAL &
ANCIENT GAME*, 1995

Most of the difficult things in golf are mental, not physical. Are subjective, not objective. Are the created phantasms of the mind, not the veritable realities of the course.

ARNOLD HAULTAIN, *THE MYSTERY OF GOLF*, 1910

The key to British links golf is the word 'frustration'. You can hit the perfect shot and, all of a sudden, it will bounce straight right or, for no apparent reason, jump beyond the hole. If I played over here four straight weeks I'd be a raving lunatic.

TOM WATSON, ON LINKS-TYPE GOLF COURSES, 1977

I don't like number 'four' balls. And I definitely don't like fives, sixes or sevens on my cards.

GEORGE ARCHER, US TOURNAMENT PRO, ON HIS SUPERSTITIONS

I say this without any reservations whatsoever. It is impossible to outplay an opponent you cannot out-think.

LAWSON LITTLE, AMERICAN PROFESSIONAL

The USGA's goal in life, at US Opens anyway, is to take players to the limit of their endurance, not physically but mentally. Frustration, fear, dashed hopes, tantrums, they are all on the USGA's wish list. And they usually get what they want through a combination of ribbon-wide fairways, five-inch rough and extremely hard and fast putting surfaces.

GOLF MONTHLY, ON THE INCREASINGLY DIFFICULT STANDARDS SET BY THE UNITED STATES GOLF ASSOCIATION IN MAJOR CHAMPIONSHIPS IN THE LATE 1990s

We are told that the great golfer is born and not made; and it is held by the best authorities that success in golf is very largely due to the possession of exactly the right temperament for the game. Generally speaking, that is a cold, phlegmatic sort of temperament, one that permits of its possessor remaining unmoved and steadily persevering towards his object in spite of a multitude of disturbing elements by which he may be surrounded, and notwithstanding the most outrageous ill-fortune with which he may be afflicted.

HENRY LEACH, *THE GOLF TEMPERAMENT*, 1899

I don't have the slightest idea; I'm not a deep thinker.

STEVE PATE, MEMBER OF THE WINNING US RYDER CUP
TEAM AT BROOKLINE IN 1999, ON THE REASONS FOR HIS
TEAM'S HISTORIC FIGHT BACK IN THE SINGLES

It has been estimated that if you laid all the golfers in the world end-to-end, they would lie indefinitely.

RICHARD SNEDDON, *THE GOLF STREAM*, 1941

....

When you go on that first tee and you're feeling bad, you know for sure that the guy you are playing is feeling just as bad.

SAM TORRANCE, EUROPEAN TOURNAMENT PROFESSIONAL,
ON THE MENTAL STRAIN OF THE RYDER CUP

....

A perfect, flowing, model style can be alarming to an opponent. The teaching of golf is not our domain: but the teaching of style comes very much into our orbit. An appearance of a strong effortless style, flowing yet built on a stable foundation, can be alarming to an opponent even if it has no effect on one's shots. Above all we recommend practising a practice swing which ends with the body turned correctly square to the direction of the ball, the hands held high, an expression of easy confidence on the face, a touch of nobility, as if one were looking towards the setting sun. Students who find themselves unable even vaguely to simulate a graceful finish may do well by going to the opposite extreme. It is possible to let go of the club almost completely at the top of the swing, recover it, and by a sort of half-paralysed jerk come down again more or less normally. Your opponent will find himself forced to stare at you, and may lose his rhythm.

STEPHEN POTTER, *THE COMPLETE GOLF GAMESMANSHIP*, 1968

He had a supernatural strength of mind.

BEN HOGAN, ON BOBBY JONES

I guess there is nothing that will get your mind off everything like golf will. I have never been depressed enough to take up the game, but they say you can get so sore at yourself that you forget to hate your enemies.

WILL ROGERS

The Art of Matchplay Golf

Stroke play is a better test of golf, but match play is a better test of character.

JOE CARR

Match play is so much more fun than stroke play.

SERGIO GARCIA, EUROPEAN RYDER CUP PLAYER

Match play, you see, is much more of a joust. It calls for a doughty, resourceful competitor, the sort of fellow who is not ruffled by his opponent's fireworks and is able to set off a few of his own when it counts.

HERBERT WARREN WIND, *AMERICAN GOLFER* MAGAZINE

I had held a notion that I could make a pretty fair appraisal of the worth of an opponent simply by speaking to him on the first tee and taking a good measuring look into his eyes.

BOBBY JONES, 1960

A good player who is a great putter is a match for any golfer. A great hitter who cannot putt is a match for no one.

BEN SAYERS, SCOTTISH PROFESSIONAL, 1890

A golf course exists primarily for match play, which is a sport, as distinguished from stroke play, which more resembles rifle shooting than a sport in that it lacks the joy of personal contact with an opponent.

FREDDIE TAIT, BRITISH AMATEUR, 1889

A secret disbelief in the enemy's play is very useful for match play.

SIR WALTER SIMPSON, *THE ART OF GOLF*, 1887

....

Let's go and kill them!

DAVID DUVAL, MEMBER OF THE WINNING US RYDER CUP TEAM IN 1999, IN AGGRESSIVE MOOD BEFORE THE SINGLES

....

In time the beginners will come to realize that as in War so in Golf, to be successful a careful study of strategy and tactics is essential. Before issuing or taking up a challenge for big stakes the player should most thoroughly investigate the characteristics and make-up of his opposite number. This involves the examination of his psychology, physiognomy and physical powers. Once satisfied in regard to these details, he may work out his plan of campaign.

H. MACNEILE DIXON, *GOLF AND HOW*, 1944

He may have gone to bed three hours ago. But he knows who he is playing. You can rest assured that he hasn't slept a wink.

LEGENDARY NIGHT OWL WALTER HAGEN, DISCUSSING HIS NEXT MATCHPLAY OPPONENT IN THE PROFESSIONAL GOLFERS ASSOCIATION CHAMPIONSHIP IN 1919

The format of the Ryder Cup was no doubt devised by somebody with shrewd sense of the sadistic.

THE DETROIT NEWS, DISCUSSING THE ULTIMATE MATCHPLAY TEAM EVENT

I didn't think you would miss it. But I wasn't going to give you the chance.

JACK NICKLAUS, CONCEDING TONY JACKLIN'S HIGHLY MISSABLE PUTT ON THE FINAL GREEN AT ROYAL BIRKDALE IN THE 1969 RYDER CUP SINGLES. ONE OF THE GREAT GOLFING GESTURES, IT ALLOWED THE ENTIRE MATCH TO BE TIED.

I've had a bad week. But in the real world, having a bad week is waking up and finding you're a steel worker in Scunthorpe.

NICK FALDO, RYDER CUP, KIAWAH ISLAND, 1991

Of all types of opponent the most irritating is, I think, 'the convenient invalid', that self-pitying monster whose hooks are the result of some galloping and mortal disease, who cannot putt because of hay-fever, who tops his mashies owing to synovitis in the elbow, is only playing because of medical advice. Then there are those opponents who say 'Bad luck' when you miss from eighteen inches, others who remark: 'Funny, I thought you'd carried that bunker for certain,' or: 'Didn't think you'd miss that one, as my ball was giving you the line.' Less trying, but somewhat embarrassing, are those who say nothing at all, till suddenly, about the eleventh tee, they snap out 'One up' or 'Three down.' Others there are who, when you are four down at the turn, and there are five couples waiting to drive off on a bleak day, begin with that dispiriting sentence: 'Last time I played this hole ...'

R. C. ROBERTSON-GLASGOW, *MORNING POST*

Don't tell the opponent to drive first (in match play) when you have won the toss for the honour. It is a confession of weakness.

H. L. FITZPATRICK, *GOLF DON'TS*, 1900

It's really two teams trying to knock seven bells out of each other.

PETER ALLISS, DESCRIBING THE HISTORY OF THE RYDER CUP

Show me a man who is a good loser and I'll show you a man who is playing golf with his boss.

ANON.

If aliens were to land and you had to pick one player to save the earth in match play, it would be Phil Mickelson.

LEE JANZEN

If ever you see a man who has tied with another for a medal, toying in the luncheon interval with a biscuit and lemon-and-soda, you may go out and bet your modest half-crown against that man with a light heart. But if you see him doctoring himself with a beefsteak and a bottle of beer, or, better still, a pint of champagne, you may go forth and back that man with as stout a heart as if you had yourself partaken of his lunch. The golfer will not do good work unless he is fed. And it is real, good, hard work that he has to do — work that will need a stout heart to do it.

HORACE HUTCHINSON, *HINTS ON MATCH AND MEDAL· PLAY*, 1899

Never was more fallacious advice given the unsuspecting golfing community, and that from one of the best golfers and best men that ever played the game. This advice has ruined many a man's game.

CHARLES BLAIR MACDONALD, RESPONDING TO HUTCHINSON'S ADVICE ALWAYS TO BET ON THE PLAYER WHO EATS A HEARTY LUNCH, 1928

I've always made a total effort, even when the odds seemed entirely against me. I never quit trying; I never felt that I didn't have a chance to win.

ARNOLD PALMER

Golf's three ugliest words: still your shot.

DAVE MARR

A gentleman at St Andrews once made a match to play level with a brother golfer who was a far stronger player than himself on the understanding only that he should be allowed to say 'Booh!' as his opponent was about to strike the ball thrice during the match. Making the most of this concession, he continually stole up behind his opponent with such disconcerting effect, that the receiver of the three 'boohs!' won the match actually without having used any of his 'boohs!' at all.

HORACE HUTCHINSON, GOLF ILLUSTRATED, 1899

Match play's the thing. Stroke play's no more than rifle-shooting.

FREDDIE TAIT, BRITISH AMATEUR CHAMPION IN 1896

I wish I was playing in the Ryder Cup team. How could they beat me? I've been struck by lightning, had two back operations, and been divorced twice.

LEE TREVINO, 1985

If your adversary is badly bunkered, there is no rule against your standing over him and counting his strokes aloud, with increasing gusto as their number mounts up; but it will be a wise precaution to arm yourself with the niblick before doing so, so as to meet him on equal terms.

HORACE HUTCHINSON, 1890

He must not think that it is a putt he would not dream of missing at the beginning of the match, or, worse still, that he missed one like it in the middle. He ought to wait calm and stupid till it is his turn to play wave back the inevitable boy who is sure to be standing behind his arm, and putt as I have told him how — neither with undue haste nor with exaggerated care. When the ball is down and the putter handed to the caddy it is not well to say, 'I couldn't have missed it.' Silence is best. The pallid cheek and trembling lip belie such braggadocio.

SIR WALTER SIMPSON, THE ART OF GOLF, 1887

Neither would I had I just been given the beating you just got.

THE REPLY GIVEN BY ERIC BROWN, AFTER HIS 4 AND 3 SINGLES VICTORY OVER THE AMERICAN TOMMY BOLT IN THE RYDER CUP AT LINDRICK IN 1957. IT SEEMS THE NOTORIOUSLY SHORT-TEMPERED BOLT HAD REFUSED TO SHAKE HANDS, SAYING HOW LITTLE HE HAD ENJOYED THE GAME.

Ballesteros can't play matchplay golf.

AN UNNAMED EUROPEAN TEAM SELECTOR, CITING THIS AS A REASON FOR LEAVING SEVE OUT OF THE 1981 RYDER CUP TEAM. PERHAPS INEVITABLY, EUROPE LOST 8–17. A FEW WEEKS LATER SEVE BEAT BEN CRENSHAW IN THE FINAL OF THE WORLD MATCHPLAY CHAMPIONSHIP AT WENTWORTH.

A secret disbelief in the enemy's play is very useful in match play.

SIR WALTER SIMPSON, THE ART OF GOLF, 1887

I play with friends, but we don't play friendly games.

BEN HOGAN

Eighteen holes of match play will teach you more about your foe than nineteen years of dealing with him across the desk.

GRANTLAND RICE, AMERICAN GOLFER MAGAZINE

One never knows when the tide at golf will turn – and turn it did. Allan warmed up and got more into his game; and then one hole was taken and another and yet another … and so on until the match stood all equal and two to play. How different the attitude of the Dunns' supporters now from their jubilant and vaunting manner at lunch time! Silence reigned, concern was on every brow. The very Dunns themselves were demoralized! On the other hand, Allan and Tom were serene, and their supporters as lively as they had been depressed before. We felt victory was ours! All this time the barometer of our expectation had been steadily rising and had now almost reached 'Set Fair!' We felt the victory was now secure: and so, in fact, it turned out, and Allan and Tom remained the victors by two holes.

H. THOMAS PETER, DESCRIBING A £400 CHALLENGE
MATCH AT NORTH BERWICK IN 1849 BETWEEN THE
CHAMPIONS OF ST ANDREWS, TOM MORRIS AND ALLAN
ROBERTSON, AND THE DUNN BROTHERS OF MUSSELBURGH,
GOLFING REMINISCENCES OF AN OLD HAND, 1890

....

Of course you may. But I ain't gonna tell ya.

BEN HOGAN, NON-PLAYING CAPTAIN OF THE 1967 US
RYDER CUP TEAM, REPLYING TO A JOURNALIST'S QUESTION,
'MAY I ASK WHY YOU HAVE PAIRED BOROS AND CASPER IN
THE FIRST MATCH?'

....

I really don't like play-offs. I feel sorry for the other guy if I win and feel worse if I lose.

CHI CHI RODRIGUEZ

If you ever feel sorry for somebody on a golf course, you better go home. If you don't kill them, they'll kill you.

SEVE BALLESTEROS

Never bet [against] anyone you meet on the first tee who has a deep suntan, a one-iron in his bag, and squinty eyes.

DAVE MARR

It is a game in which the whole temperamental strength of one side is hurled against the strength of the other, and the two human natures are pressing bitterly and relentlessly against each other from the first moment of the game to the last. It is the whole man, mind and body. That is the meaning of the temperamental factor in golf, and that is why a great match at golf is great indeed.

HENRY LEACH, *GREAT GOLFERS IN THE MAKING*, 1907

Of course in every match your ultimate success will depend largely upon the terms on which you have arranged to play before starting. The settling of these conditions is sometimes a nice matter, needing all the wisdom of the serpent in combination with the meekness of the dove. At such times you will perhaps be surprised to hear a person, whom personally you had previously believed to somewhat overrate his game, now speaking of it in terms of the greatest modesty.

HORACE HUTCHINSON, *HINTS ON GOLF*, 1899

The Caddie

There were three things in the world that he held in the smallest esteem: slugs, poets and caddies with hiccups.

P. G. WODEHOUSE

From men who have adopted carrying as a trade, the golfer is entitled to expect the highest standard of efficiency. If he carries for you regularly, he ought to know what club you intend to take, and to give it without being asked. When you are in doubt about how to play your shot, he ought to confirm you in the opinion you have formed regarding it. [But above all] he must never show the just contempt he has for your game.

SIR WALTER SIMPSON, *THE ART OF GOLF*, 1887

I don't think anywhere is there a symbiotic relationship between caddie and player like there is in golf.

JOHNNY MILLER

There is a miscellaneous selection of caddies: boys, ragamuffins just out of prison, workmen out of a job, and professional carriers. All but the last ought to be avoided.

SIR WALTER SIMPSON, *THE ART OF GOLF*, 1887

Caddies are a breed unto themselves and they certainly earn their wage for humping this lot around four miles of land.

DAI REES, FORMER BRITISH RYDER CUP CAPTAIN

The duties of the caddie are manifold, including the responsibilities of preceptor, doctor and lawyer. He will be called upon to devise means of escape from soul-trying bunkers, administer to the wounded pride of the unsuccessful, and turn legislator at a crowded teeing-ground.

C. W. WHITNEY, AMERICAN WRITER, 1894

There is at Edinburgh a society or corporation of errand-boys, called Cawdies, who ply in the streets at night with paper lanterns, and are very serviceable in carrying messages. These fellows, though shabby in their appearance, and rudely familiar in their address, are wonderfully acute, and so noted for fidelity, that there is no instance of a cawdy's having betrayed his trust. Such is their intelligence, that they know, not only every individual of the place, but also every stranger, by the time he has been four-and-twenty hours in Edinburgh; and no transaction, even the most private, can escape their notice.

TOBIAS SMOLLETT, ON LETTER CARRIERS WHO LATER BECAME CADDIES, *THE EXPEDITION OF HUMPHRY CLINKER*, 1771

Experienced and more respectful caddies wore boots and stockings stood aloof outside the gate. These were engaged by the best players and received sixpence, maybe, and two-pence for club cleaning. In neither case were the fees paid until the clubs had been delivered at the back door of the Clubhouse, the steelheads properly polished with emery cloth.

ROBERT HARRIS, *SIXTY YEARS OF GOLF*, 1953

Friends noticed that the caddie always walked barefoot. It was his duty when [Errol] Flynn's ball went in the rough, to pick it up with his unusually long toes and, without stooping down, deposit it quietly on the fairway.

NEW YORKER, 1937

I am only about a ten-handicap as a magician; you have to do a half-hour show at one of their monthly meetings. I taught myself from books, and I have a good friend who is training to be a magician. I like small tricks, close-up stuff. I don't saw my caddie in half if he gives me a bad club!

DENNIS EDLUND, EUROPEAN TOUR PROFESSIONAL, EXPLAINING WHY HE WAS CONTEMPLATING JOINING THE MAGIC CIRCLE IN SWEDEN, 1998

My usual caddie, Flinn, is one of the same lot. He carries well, knows his employer's game, and almost never needs to be asked for a club – he has always the right one ready. His employer's clubs he keeps in good order. He is always sober during the day – at least, nearly always.

J. KERR, *GOLF*, 1893

We're not the show; the player is. Tiger has taken the world by storm, and I'm out there with him. He's been wonderful. He is wonderful. But my life hasn't changed that much. I get a little more attention now, that's all.

MIKE 'FLUFF' COWAN, ON CADDYING FOR TIGER WOODS

I had had, ever since I had been at Sandwich, one of the worst caddies it had ever been my misfortune to be saddled with. This young man, about twenty-six years old, was a natural born idiot, and cross-eyed at that.

WALTER J. TRAVIS, *THE AMERICAN GOLFER*, 1910

No man can play at golf who has not a servant at command to assist him. It is probable that no sport exists in the world today or ever did exist in which the services of a paid assistant are an essential as in this national game of Scotland.

HORACE HUTCHINSON, 1899

....

Do I every disagree with him on course strategy? Never – unless he's wrong.

GARY NICKLAUS, ON CADDYING FOR HIS FATHER JACK

....

Were some of the players to carry their own dubs, I think they would find it almost as good exercise as the playing, and, methinks, the sheaf of sticks would grow beautifully less, and they would soon discover that they could do all that was necessary with four instruments.

LEAMINGTON SPA ADVERTISER, 1899

The only time I talk on a golf course is to my caddie – and only then to complain when he gives me the wrong club.

SEVE BALLESTEROS

I'm trim as a daisy. I've just finished a bottle of brandy and will start on the next one when you've won this tournament.

MAX FAULKNER'S CADDIE DURING THE NEWS OF THE WORLD TOURNAMENT IN THE 1950S. HAVING MADE A BIRDIE, FAULKNER NOTICED HIS CADDIE WAS FLAT OUT ON THE SIDE OF THE GREEN HOLDING THE FLAGSTICK. HE THEN CALMLY REPLACED THE FLAG IN THE HOLE, DRAGGED THE SLEEPING CADDIE BEHIND A GORSE BUSH AND CARRIED ON WITH HIS GAME.

At home a caddie's function is to act as one's mentor, guide, spiritual adviser, and beast of burden, but in countries where a second is employed, known as a something wallah – I regret my knowledge of Oriental-languages prevents my being more explicit – he marches ahead of the player, at some distance decided by himself, according to whether he is an optimist or a pessimist by nature.

H. MACNEILE DIXON, GOLF AND HOW, 1944

The life of a professional golfer is precarious at best. Win, and they carry you to the clubhouse on their shoulders. Lose, and you pay the caddies in the dark.

GENE SARAZEN

On another occasion I saw a caddie walk along the semi-rough and him boot the ball a good 20 yards. This particular caddie had been in the pioneer corps in France during the war. There was no question that these caddies were doing it because the pro might slip them some money; they just did it for the devil of it.

MAX FAULKNER ON TOURNAMENT GOLF IN THE 1950S

I wanted to see golf from inside the ropes.

FANNY SUNESSON ON HER REASONS FOR CADDYING

I don't know why that putt hung on the edge. I'm a clean liver. It must be my caddie.

JOANNE CARNER, AMERICAN LPGA PROFESSIONAL, 1980S

When Langer practises on his own, he can hold up a four-ball.

DAVE MUSGROVE, HIS LONG-TIME CADDIE, ON THE GERMAN'S PRE-TOURNAMENT PREPARATION

The province of the 'caddy' in the game is to follow his master as closely as possible, generally at a dead run, and be ready to hand him whichever implement of the game the master calls for, as the play may demand. For instance the ball may fall in such a way that it is lodged an inch or two above the ground, having fallen in thick grass. The player, rushing up to it, calls on his 'caddy' for a baffing spoon, and having received it from the hands of his servant he bats the ball with the spoon in the direction of the hole. An inviolable rule of the game is that no player shall touch the ball from one limit of the circle to the other with his hands. All play must be done with the tools. In this the caddy really gets about as much exercise out of the sport as his master, and he must be so familiar with the tools of the game that he can hand out the right implement at any moment when it is called for.

The Philadelphia Times, 1889

My game is so bad I gotta hire three caddies – one to walk the left rough, one for the right rough, and one down the middle. And the one in the middle doesn't have much to do.

Dave Hill, former US Ryder Cup player

I was lying tenth and had a 35-foot putt. I whispered over my shoulder: 'How does this one break?' And my caddie said, 'Who cares?'

Jack Lemmon

Caddies are a breed of their own. If you shoot 66, they say, 'Man, we shot sixty-six!' But go out and shoot 77 and they say, 'Hell, he shot seventy-seven!'

Lee Trevino

....

I know you can get fined for throwing a club. What I want to know is if you can get fined for throwing a caddie.

Tommy Bolt

....

Nobody but you and your caddie cares what you do out there, and if your caddie is betting against you, he doesn't care either.

Lee Trevino

If I needed advice from my caddie, he'd be hitting the shots and I'd be carrying the bag.

BOBBY JONES

Ah! what bitter men are we golfers! How selfish in our thoughts! How petty in our little strifes! Day after day we wage our insignificant battles, curse our fate, as we smile with wan politeness; loathe our beastly opponent, his wretched, sniffing caddie, and his intolerable new set of irons.

R. C. ROBERTSON-GLASGOW, *MORNING POST*

Don't worry about your caddie. He may be an irritating little wretch, but for eighteen holes he is your caddie.

ARNOLD HAULTAIN, *THE MYSTERY OF GOLF*, 1910

The caddies wanted to raise some cash to buy softball equipment to help pass the long hours on tour. I told them, 'Well, guys, if I win the Dinah Shore, I'll buy your softball equipment.' So I said, 'Now you know what to do with your players. Let me win the tournament!' In the end, I guess I didn't need their help.

NANCY LOPEZ, IN HUMOROUS MOOD, SHORTLY AFTER WINNING THE 1981 DINAH SHORE

With reference to the reported world's record rebound of a golf ball from the head of a Scotch caddie which appeared in the home golfing papers, I beg to inform you that whilst playing the 7th hole at the Premier Mine course (Transvaal) on 28th September, my ball struck a native caddie (who was standing 150 yards away at the side of a tree just off the line of the fairway) on the forehead just above the right eye. The drive in question was one of those so dear to a golfer, a hard raking shot. The ball – a Colonel – rebounded back in a direct line 75 yards (distance measured). Strange to relate, but beyond a slight abrasion of the skin, the native was not affected at all. Therefore, you will readily observe that the record of the Scotsman is easily outclassed.

EDWARD STANWARD, IN A LETTER TO *GOLF MONTHLY*, CLAIMING A RATHER UNUSUAL DISTANCE RECORD, 1914

On parts of the Continent female caddies are much in evidence, probably due to the natural desire of the inhabitants to find employment for their surplus female population.

H. MACNEILE DIXON, *GOLF AND HOW*, 1944

My caddie told me he was getting blisters from raking so much.

JOANNE CARNER, AFTER ONE VISIT TOO MANY TO THE SAND DURING A TOURNAMENT ROUND IN THE 1970S

When I ask you what club to use, look the other way and don't answer.

SAM SNEAD TO HIS CADDIE

Why ask me? You've asked me two times already and paid no attention to what I said. So pick your own goddam club!

DOW FINSTERWALD'S CADDIE DURING THE US OPEN AT CHERRY HILLS, 1960

Golf – the Exasperating Game

One reason golf is such an exasperating game is that a thing we learned is so easily forgotten, and we find ourselves struggling year after year with faults we had discovered and corrected time and again.

BOBBY JONES

Golf puts a man's character on the anvil and his richest qualities – patience, poise, restraint – to the flame.

BILLY CASPER

The most exquisitely satisfying act in the world of golf is that of throwing a club. The full backswing, the delayed wrist action, the flowing follow-through, followed by that unique whirring sound, reminiscent only of a passing flock of starlings, are without parallel in sport.

HENRY LONGHURST

He regarded those playing around him as natural enemies and idiots, and once, when he missed a very short putt, he yelled down an adjoining fairway: 'D—n you, sir! Do you mind not flashing your brassy like that while I am putting?' On the tees during his practice swings the herbaceous vandalism was frightful to see; but, as the fids of turf spurted into the air, his comment would be, 'Club much too long – can't make it out,' or, 'Dropping the right shoulder again.'

R. C. ROBERTSON-GLASGOW, MORNING POST

The poetic temperament is the worst for golf. It dreams of brilliant drives, iron shots laid dead, and long putts holed, while in real golf success waits for him who takes care of the foozles and leaves the fine shots to take care of themselves.

SIR WALTER SIMPSON

....

What goes up must come down. But don't expect it to come down where you can find it.

LILY TOMLIN, AMERICAN ACTRESS

....

The game is not as easy as it seems. In the first place, the terrible inertia of the ball must be overcome.

LORD WELLWOOD, 1895

A sight that has been seen at Westward Ho! [Royal North Devon Golf Club] is that of a gallant Colonel stripping himself to the state in which Nature gave him to an admiring world, picking his way daintily with unshod feet over the great boulders of the Pebble Ridge, and when he came to the sea, wading out as far as possible, and hurling forth, one after the other, beyond the line of the farthest breakers the whole set of his offending clubs. That the waves and the tide were sure to bring them in again, to the delight of the salvaging caddies, made no matter to him. From him they were gone for ever and his soul was at rest.

HORACE HUTCHINSON, *FIFTY YEARS OF GOLF*, 1914

The glorious thing is that thousands of golfers, in park land, on windy downs, in gorse, in heather, by the many-sounding seas, enjoy their imbecilities, revel in their infirmities, and from failure itself draw that final victory – the triumph of hope.

R. C. ROBERTSON-GLASGOW

I don't enjoy playing video golf because there is nothing to throw.

PAUL AZINGER

No matter what happens, never give up a hole ... In tossing in your cards after a bad beginning you also undermine your whole game, because to quit between tee and green is more habit-forming than drinking a highball before breakfast.

SAM SNEAD

I doubt if we in America will ever be able to extract so much pleasure from it. Our dispositions, our temperaments, are not golf-like; we hurry through life at too rapid a gait; we have not the time to give golf in order to gain that responsive charm the game holds for the leisurely suitor.

C. W. WHITNEY, *HARPERS MONTHLY MAGAZINE*, 1894

If there is any larceny in a man, golf will bring it out.

PAUL GALLICO

Your ego is everything. And if you don't get that pumped up regularly you can't last.

DAVE MARR

Golf, like measles, should be caught young, for, if postponed to riper years, the results may be serious.

P. G. WODEHOUSE

Golf increases the blood pressure, ruins the disposition, spoils the digestion, induces Neurasthenia, hurts the eyes, calluses the hands, ties kinks in the nervous system, debauches the morals, drives men to drink or homicide, breaks up the family, turns the ductless glands into internal warts, corrodes the pneumo-gastric nerve, breaks off the edges of the vertebrae, induces spinal meningitis and progressive mendacity, and starts angina pectoris.

DR A. S. LAMB

There is one man who ought never appear on a golfing green. And this is the good man. Let him remain away. That immaculate creature whose life is spent in seeing his neighbour's faults and comparing them with his own wonderful perfection, is quite out of place amongst golfers. They are all men, not saints. Therefore let the Pharisee, whose pretensions to superiority we will never dispute, keep at home.

DR PROUDFOOT, 1890

Lie? I've got no f—ing lie. I don't even have a f—ing shot!

AN IRATE MILLER BARBER, WHEN ASKED BY COMMENTATOR
KEN VENTURI ABOUT HIS LIE DURING THE FINAL ROUND OF
THE CBS GOLF CLASSIC

Pick the ball up, have the clubs destroyed, and leave the course.

ADVICE FROM VISCOUNT CASTLEROSSE TO HIS CADDIE
AFTER TOPPING THREE CONSECUTIVE SHOTS, 1930s

If you pick up a golfer and hold it close to your ear, like a conch shell, and listen – you will hear an alibi.

FRED BECK

The angry golfer has been known to relieve his pent-up feelings by hurling his club far from him after the failure of his stroke. This is an extremely dangerous habit, as, in his anger, the golfer is frequently careless of the direction in which his club flies, and his partner will do well to keep an eye on his movements.

GARDEN C. SMITH, *THE WORLD OF GOLF*, 1898

Golf does strange things to other people too. It makes liars out of honest men, cheats out of altruists, cowards out of brave men, and fools out of everybody.

MILTON GROSS, AMERICAN GOLF JOURNALIST

Baseball reveals character; golf exposes it.

ERNIE BANKS, TOP US BASEBALL PROFESSIONAL OF THE
1960s

The only way of really finding out a man's true character is to play golf with him. In no other walk of life does the cloven hoof so quickly display itself.

P. G. WODEHOUSE

If you watch a game, it's fun. If you play it, it's recreation. If you work at it, it's golf.

BOB HOPE

The fairways get longer and the holes get smaller.

BOBBY LOCKE, FINDING GOLF A LITTLE TOUGHER AS HE APPROACHED HIS 60TH BIRTHDAY

Golf is a test of temper, a trial of honour, a revealer of character. It affords a chance to play the man and act the gentleman. It means going out into God's out-of-doors, getting close to nature, fresh air, exercise, a sweeping away of the mental cobwebs. It is a cure for care – an antidote to worry. It includes companionship with friends, social intercourse, opportunities for courtesy, kindliness and generosity to an opponent. It promotes not only physical health but moral force.

DAVID ROBERTSON FORGAN, 1898

I believe you know something about a game called Golf. Some people here object to it being called a game, and prefer to designate it a science. I should term it a disease, or even an epidemic.

ANONYMOUS LETTER TO *GOLF ILLUSTRATED* MAGAZINE, 1901

Like most professional golfers, I have a tendency to remember my poor shots a shade more vividly than the good ones.

BEN HOGAN

It's good to be reminded of how this game is. Anything can go wrong for anybody. Sometimes when you get on a roll, you tend to forget that.

DAVID DUVAL, STUMBLING TO WEEKEND ROUNDS OF 78–76
IN THE 1999 HOUSTON OPEN, HAVING ALREADY WON
FOUR US TOUR TITLES AND $2.7 MILLION IN PRIZE MONEY
AND BECOME WORLD NUMBER ONE IN THE SAME SEASON

Golf is not a mere game; it is a disease, infectious and contagious, which once acquired cannot be shaken off. Once a golfer always a golfer – there's no help for it!

L. LATCHFORD, *THE YOUNG MAN*, 1903

Right after I hit, some guy in the gallery yells out that I was a wuss for laying up! I'm leading the tournament and he's outside the ropes. Who understands better how to play the hole? I have 13 years' experience of when you lay up and when you don't. I'm just not going to put up with it.

DAVIS LOVE III, ON THE ABUSE HE RECEIVED AFTER LAYING
UP AT A DIFFICULT PAR-FIVE HOLE DURING A PGA TOUR
EVENT, 1999

Of all the games in which the soul of the Anglo-Saxon delights, there is perhaps none which is a severer test of that mysterious quality called 'nerve' than the game of golf.

HORACE HUTCHINSON, *GOLF*, 1890

The biggest liar in the world is the golfer who claims that he plays the game merely for exercise.

TOMMY BOLT

Great champions learn from past experiences, whether those be good or bad. A lot of times a guy needs to be knocked down before he gets up and fights.

PAUL AZINGER

With golf you can never get it right. If you work hard on the range to get things right, then you are automatically neglecting other things.

NICK FALDO

Despite having the added benefit of no one else to hamper your progress, no other game offers so much potential for failure.

A. J. DALCONEN, GOLF: THE HISTORY OF THE ROYAL & ANCIENT GAME, 1995

I recall the sad case of a friend of mine who, during a round, unfortunately sliced his ball into a neighbouring fairway, striking at the same time an Oriental gentleman playing the adjoining hole. My friend went across to apologize for the accident and at the same time to play his ball. The Oriental gentleman, having recognized my friend as the unprovoked aggressor, with true Bushido chivalry, bowed to his caddie, demanded his niblick, and shouting 'Banzai' advanced and felled my unfortunate friend with a well-placed swing over the right ear. History does not relate the fate of the yellow invader, but it is believed that, honour being satisfied, he committed hari-kiri in the bunker behind the 14th green. My friend never recovered from the shock of losing both ear and match at one and the same time, though admittedly he never sliced again.

H. MacNeile Dixon, *Golf and How*, 1944

Yes, it is a cruel game, one in which the primitive instincts of man are given full play, and the difference between golf and fisticuffs is that in one the pain is of the mind and in the other it is of the body.

Henry Leach, 1905

I've just discovered the great secret of golf. You can't play a really hot game unless you're so miserable that you don't worry over yourshots. Look at the top-notchers. Have you ever seen a happy pro?

P. G. Wodehouse

I was aggressive. I was defensive. Then I was gone.

Steve Jones, former US Open Champion, on a poor round of 78 in the 1997 US Masters at Augusta

Golf is a lot of walking, broken up by disappointment and bad arithmetic.

Earl Wilson, member of the British House of Lords

Every morning lawyers who are neglecting their clients, doctors who have forgotten their patients, businessmen who have sacrificed their affairs, even ministers of the gospel who have forsaken their churches gather in the noisy dressing room and listen with servile attention while some unscrubbed boy who goes around under eighty imparts a little of his miraculous knowledge. Two hours later, for every ten that have gone out so blithely, two return crushed and despondent, denouncing and renouncing the game, once and for all, absolutely and finally until the afternoon, when they return like thieves in the night and venture out in a desperate hope; two more come stamping back in even more offensive enthusiasm; and the remainder straggle home moody and disillusioned, reviving their sunken spirits by impossible tales of past accomplishments.

OWEN JOHNSON, *EVEN THREES*, 1912

In golf, more than any other sport, to travel hopefully is better than to arrive.

ROBERT BROWNING, ENGLISH WRITER

No other game requires such a variety of physical and mental adjustments, and no other game gives so complete a measure of the whole man.

CHARLES STEDMAN HANKS, AMERICAN WRITER, 1903

It is a game of hard rubs and annoyances, a game of which the exasperations no less than the fascinations were never better summarized than in these words of the grand old golfer: 'It's aye fechtin' against ye.'

HORACE HUTCHINSON, *HINTS ON MATCH AND MEDAL PLAY*, 1899

Golf is the hardest sport. One day you're up on cloud nine and the next day you couldn't scratch a whale's belly.

SAM SNEAD

Golf from its own peculiar character of sport requires a large variety of implements called clubs to move, by devious and dextrous hits, a very small ball through an adventurous journey, over undulating ground, from a starting place called the 'tee' into a hole of irritatingly small dimensions cut in the turf.

ROBERT HARRIS, *SIXTY YEARS OF GOLF*, 1953

To play golf is the search for perfection. A seemingly endless struggle to attain the unattainable. It requires a complete mastery over emotion, nerve and temper with success or failure depending on the individual's ability to handle all three at once. After all, in what other game are you expected to summon up the ability to drive a stationary ball with the force of a sledgehammer one moment, then chip it with the delicacy of a surgeon the next?

A. J. DALCONEN, *GOLF: THE HISTORY OF THE ROYAL & ANCIENT GAME*, 1995

The game of golf has, as I have previously made clear, its peculiarities and perplexities, and the passions released during its performance, from club wrecking to suicidal impulses, have induced its Directors to introduce an extra hole, known as the Nineteenth, played rather differently to those preceding it.

H. MACNEILE DIXON, *GOLF AND HOW*, 1944

....

I'm playing better now than I ever have in my career. I don't know what's happened, but I'm not going to search for the answer.

RAY FLOYD, SHORTLY AFTER WINNING THE DORAL-EASTERN OPEN, 1981

On a day in April, I walked round the Links with a foursome; the only time I ever did so. It is sad to make such a confession: but truth must be told. My brother Alexander and Lord Colin Campbell played against Tulloch and a golfer departed. It was extraordinary how peppery the golfers became. Tulloch and his partner were being badly beaten, and became demoralized. Tulloch, seeing his partner doing something stupid, made some suggestion to him. On which his irate friend brandished his club in the air, and literally yelled out, 'No directions! I'll take no directions!'

A. H. BOYD, *TWENTY-FIVE YEARS OF ST ANDREWS*, 1892

I'm too young to get fried up out here – I don't like the game that much.

FUZZY ZOELLER, ON WHY HE WALKED OFF THE COURSE
DURING A THUNDER STORM IN 1983

He would arrive, with erratic, curse-these-golf-club-garages swerves, on to the scene, give me a passing glare, disappear into the dressing-room, from which emerged sounds like a boot-fight between customer and assistant on a sale-day then dash to the first tee. There he would allow me a curt nod of recognition, and shout such single comments as 'Off as soon as possible – late – course overcrowded – too many women – shouldn't play at all – talk to the secretary ...' I have, indeed, known him to tee his ball in front of three waiting pairs, drive it off, and expect me to do the same. In others this would be accounted rude; in him it was natural, even magnificent.

R. C. ROBERTSON-GLASGOW, *MORNING POST*

I said a few unprintable words under my breath and called it a mulligan.

ALAN SHEPARD, US ASTRONAUT, ON HIS MISHIT SIX-IRON ON THE MOON, 1971

As I told 'em, 'If you want to laugh, you have two choices: either go to a circus or I'll bury this eight-iron in your head.'

DAVID GRAHAM'S REACTION TO HECKLING FANS AT THE 1981 BRITISH OPEN AT ROYAL ST GEORGE'S

Don't worry about it. Everybody has bad days. The chairman of the board has bad days. Multimillionaires have bad days. Even the Pope has bad days.

HERMAN MITCHELL, OFFERING A FEW WORDS OF COMFORT TO HIS EMPLOYER, LEE TREVINO, IN 1982

In this weather golf is not a game, it is a form of torture.

FRED PIGNON, MANAGER OF THE 1931 BRITISH RYDER CUP TEAM, DESCRIBING THE PROBLEMS HIS PLAYERS FACED AT SCIOTO COUNTRY CLUB, COLUMBUS, IN THE BOILING HEAT OF AN AMERICAN SUMMER

Don't lose your temper about anything – anything whatsoever. If you lose your temper, you lose everything – self control, self respect, judgement, equanimity, decency of language, and, of course, the hole, and probably the game.

ARNOLD HAULTAIN, THE MYSTERY OF GOLF, 1910

No game demands more scientific accuracy than golf, and there is no game in which shots that are not well played more surely meet with their just punishment. In the reverse there is no game in which small degrees of skill count more regularly in favour of the man who possesses them.

JAMES BRAID, HOW TO PLAY GOLF, 1901

I'm going to miss at least seven shots in every 18 holes of golf I play, so if I'm going to be angry, I may as well start on the first tee.

WALTER HAGEN

I am no golfer. Indeed, I once made myself unpopular by referring to the game as 'outdoor tiddleywinks'.

McDONALD HASTINGS

It has often been a mystery to me men play golf at all, for if they are not at the top of their game and winning their matches they become so depressed it is a misery to play with them. One gets the feeling that one must miss a few shots in order to try and bring about a more pleasant state of affairs.

S. MURE FERGUSSON, TOP BRITISH AMATEUR, 1914

I'm hitting the ball like a damn polka dancer – first off the heel, then off the toe.

ANDREW KIRKALDY, OLD-TIME SCOTTISH PROFESSIONAL, 1900

The awful thing about socketing is its unexpectedness. Suddenly, perhaps after months of relief, the traitorous thought, 'I might socket this one', comes to mind. On occasions like this the mind turns powerfully to the preventives, but as anxiety mounts, so does the body fail to respond to instructions. The weight is thrust back on the heels, the right elbow is tucked in and the club held loosely, but by now the wretched mind is a stir with inhibitions. In the desire to get the shot over, one is undone and there is the ball, hurtling knee high to cover-point. The socket is especially cruel, for invariably it costs more than one stroke. Even if recovery be possible, the mind by then is perfectly conditioned to socket again. From visualizing a pretty pitch nestling by the hole, with a possible putt for three, one is condemned in a trice to struggling desperately for a five or worse. And the whole performance is so ignominious.

P. A. WARD-THOMAS, BRITISH GOLF WRITER

I am still undecided as to which of these two is the hardest shot in golf for me – any unconceded putt, or the explosion shot off the first tee. Both have caused me more strokes than I care to write about.

RING LARDNER, AMERICAN WRITER

I have been playing golf three hundred and seventy-five years and, after all that time, I finally reach the day where I ask a 25-year-old caddie what club to use.

BOBBY CRUIKSHANK, AFTER MAKING DOUBLE BOGEY IN THE FINAL ROUND OF THE US OPEN AT OAKLAND HILLS, 1924

Money
and Golf

I never wanted to be a millionaire; I just wanted to live like one.
WALTER HAGEN

Victory is everything. You can spend the money, but you can never spend the memories.
KEN VENTURI

Why pay dues at a club for the privilege of working yourself into a fury? Get your money's worth!
FRANK C. TONE, *THE AMERICAN*, 1928

Golf has never had a showman like him. All the professionals who have a chance to go after the big money today should say a silent thanks to Walter each time they stretch a cheque between their fingers.
GENE SARAZEN, 1950

Hale Irwin isn't the sort of golfer who celebrates victories by buying champagne for the house. His idea of a party is drinking a sugar-free cola and contemplating prudent ways of investing his latest pay cheque.

FRED GUZMAN, SAN JOSÉ MERCURY NEWS, 1984

Yes, I had a really great par at the fifth.

ANDREW CARNEGIE, RESPONDING TO THE
CONGRATULATIONS OF SOMEONE ON THE SAME DAY HE SOLD
HIS STEEL BUSINESS FOR $250 MILLION

I don't think golfers are all that highly paid. Besides the actual money didn't enter my head when I was out on the course. Anyway, once the taxman, my agent and my caddie have all had their share, then we are down to about $400,000.

BARRY LANE, SHORTLY AFTER PICKING UP A $1 MILLION
CHEQUE FOR WINNING THE INAUGURAL ANDERSON
CONSULTING CHAMPIONSHIP, 1995

Yes, you're probably right about the left hand, but the fact is that I take the cheques with my right hand.

BOBBY LOCKE, SOUTH AFRICAN PROFESSIONAL, ON HIS
WEAK LEFT-HAND GRIP

You know, someday somebody's gonna come out here and tee it up nude.

BOB WYNN, FORMER TOURNAMENT PROFESSIONAL, ON
ENDORSEMENT MONEY, 1975

More money. Otherwise, no difference. Birdie the same. Par the same. Bogey the same. Out-of-bounds the same.

SEVE BALLESTEROS, ON THE DIFFERENCE BETWEEN THE AMERICAN TOUR AND EUROPE

I may buy the Alamo and give it back to Mexico.

LEE TREVINO, ASKED WHAT HE'D DO WITH HIS RECORD WINNINGS IN 1968

Is winning the Open worth a million pounds? Well, it's certainly worthwhile winning it — I would recommend it to anybody.

SANDY LYLE, BRITISH OPEN CHAMPION IN 1985

They're going to make a lot of money when they cut and bale the hay out there.

PAYNE STEWART, ON THE ROUGH AT CARNOUSTIE FOR THE 1999 BRITISH OPEN

Walter Hagen was the first player I knew that earned $1 million from golf, and of course he spent it, too. Sam Snead earned $1 million, too — and he saved $2 million.

FRED CORCORAN, AMERICAN GOLFING ENTREPRENEUR

For that kind of money, I'd wear a skirt.

JIMMY DEMARET, WHEN ASKED TO WEAR A NUMBER ON HIS BACK DURING A TOURNAMENT IN CALIFORNIA

There goes 100,000 bucks!

AL WATROUS, WATCHING BOBBY JONES PULL AWAY IN THE
FINAL STAGES OF THE BRITISH OPEN AT ROYAL LYTHAM IN
1926

The only stats I care about are pay cheques and victories.

GREG NORMAN

You make a lot of money in this game. Just ask my ex-wives.
Both of them are so rich that neither of their husbands work.

LEE TREVINO

I don't know what the plan is tonight, but I'm pretty sure I will
be buying.

DAVID DUVAL, ABOUT A SMALL PARTY CELEBRATING THE
FACT THAT HE HAD JUST FINISHED NUMBER ONE IN THE US
PGA MONEY LIST FOR 1998 WITH EARNINGS OF
$2,591,031

Hey, if I'm dumb enough to lose a piece of paper worth
$40,000 on a bar, do you think I can remember what year it
was?

ROGER MALTBIE, AMERICAN TOUR PLAYER, ABOUT WINNING
A GOLF TOURNAMENT BUT MISPLACING THE CHEQUE

I always travel first class. That way I think first class and I'm
more likely to play first class.

RAY FLOYD, DESCRIBING HOW HE GETS THROUGH MORE
THAN $50,000 A YEAR IN TRAVELLING EXPENSES

Every kid learning how to play golf dreams about winning the Masters, about winning the Open, not about being the leading money winner. I've never short changed myself on dreams.

Tom Kite

I can always dig ditches.

Arnold Palmer, explaining to manager Mark McCormack what he could do if he lost all his money

I made $700 for winning my first US Open and $500 for the British Open. Today a good, young golfer doesn't have to be a champion. He gets $150,000 for wearing a logo on his cap or his sleeve.

Gary Player, on prize money in the modern game, 1998

If you don't mind, Mr Crosby, I'd rather have cash.

Sam Snead, on being presented with a $500 cheque for winning the Bing Crosby Pro-Am

I'm on steak now. With $200,000 a year, ain't no sense in eating rice and beans any more.

Chi Chi Rodriguez, answering reporters who accused him of putting on a few pounds, 1970

I would rather die owing a million than owning a million.

Eric Brown, former British Ryder Cup captain, on his philosophy in life

The most competitive product South Korea has ever shipped abroad.

A SPOKESMAN FOR SAMSUNG, WHO AWARDED SE RI PAK A $296,000 BONUS FOR WINNING THE US WOMEN'S OPEN, CLAIMING THE AIR TIME SHE HAD PROVIDED WAS WORTH MORE THAN $100 MILLION

Let's see, I think right now I'm third in the money winning and first in money spending.

'CHAMPAGNE' TONY LEMA

We're paupers in a millionaires' playground.

DAI REES, BRITISH RYDER CUP CAPTAIN, ON THE ELDORADO COUNTRY CLUB, CALIFORNIA, THE VENUE FOR THE 1959 RYDER CUP

However often you have won, and however much money you have made, you still get nervous over those closing holes. The only difference is that you learn to handle it better. Above all, you think more clearly under pressure.

NICK PRICE

I guess the reason I enjoy playing cards is that you have to think about what you're doing. You play the right hands and get rewarded for your patience. You have to wait for the streaks. When you're winning, you have to go with your own luck. In golf it goes the same way. The way I play cards is exactly the way I play golf. The only difference is how much I win.

BOB TWAY, FORMER UNITED STATES PGA CHAMPION, ON THE SIMILARITIES BETWEEN GOLF AND PLAYING CARDS

I'm going to win so much this year that even my caddie will make it into the top twenty money winners' list.

LEE TREVINO, IN CONFIDENT MOOD GOING INTO THE 1973 GOLF SEASON

The guys I'll never understand are the self-confessed non-competitors – the golfers who pick up $100,000 plus a year without ever winning a tournament and go around telling the world how happy they are to finish ninth every week.

JACK NICKLAUS, TALKING ABOUT THE WILL TO WIN

These guys are looking to get a good pay day with as little hassle as possible. Well sorry, Jimmy, but this is The Open, the tournament. It's the big exam.

JOHN PHILP, HEAD GREENKEEPER AT CARNOUSTIE, THE VENUE FOR THE 1999 CHAMPIONSHIP

I played so bad, I got a get-well card from the IRS.

JOHNNY MILLER

I cannot find a job that pays me $700,000 a year, so, until I do, I'll be right here.

PAT BRADLEY, AMERICAN LPGA PROFESSIONAL

Pasta can be aggressive or mild, like Greg.

A MARKETING SPOKESMAN FOR GREG NORMAN PASTA SAUCES, 1998. WITH A LARGE ITALIAN COMMUNITY IN AUSTRALIA, THE PASTA SAUCE MARKET IS WORTH CLOSE TO $100 MILLION.

In a Major championship you don't care about the money. You're just trying to get your name on a piece of silver.

NICK FALDO

I like the thought of playing for money instead of silverware. I never did like to polish.

PATTY SHEEHAN, LPGA MEMBER, ON TURNING PROFESSIONAL

I wouldn't want Tiger's life, even if it does bring things like a $40 million Nike contract. It's not worth it. I can go out for a drink with my mates and no one bothers me, and that's how I like it. I would never want bodyguards, all that hassle.

LEE WESTWOOD, ON THE COMPARATIVE OBSCURITY OF PLAYING ON THE EUROPEAN TOUR

They are looking long term. I think they want to bring out a weight loss pill.

LEE WESTWOOD, ON WHY A VITAMIN COMPANY WANTED TO SPONSOR HIM

Even my next-door neighbour talks to me now.

CHRIS MOODY, AFTER PICKING UP £65,000 FOR WINNING THE 1988 EUROPEAN MASTERS AT WALTON HEATH

Winning used to be the important thing. The money was nice to have, but it was not the most important thing. Today, the American player doesn't have that strong desire to win any more, he has the strong desire to win all this money.

RAY FLOYD, ON THE RISING LEVEL OF PRIZE MONEY ON OFFER IN 1989

Sure the purses are obscene. The average worker, let's say, makes $25,000 a year, while a golfer makes $25,000 for finishing 10th. Our values have departed somewhat.

TOM WATSON, ALSO ON PRIZE MONEY, 1989

···

Here we are, making thousands of dollars a year, and we're trying to change our swings.

JOHNNY MILLER, ON THE PRACTICE GROUND, 1974

···

People often ask me if I get any fun out of playing golf, and the answer is 'Yes'. I do get a lot of fun out of playing. Of course, winning big prizes is most important, for playing golf is my living; but if I were to think only of the money and worry about not winning, I think I should climb up the wall.

PETER ALLISS

They used to play the Robinson fall Classic in Robinson, Illinois. Errol Flynn couldn't get laid in Robinson, Illinois, with a two-million-dollar bill.

JOHN JACOBS, US TOUR PROFESSIONAL, 1975

I just shot 85 and I still don't know what happened. I teach at a little club in Minnesota. I had to cancel my lessons to get here. I practised all week and the members were very nice to me. It cost me $400 just to come here. I'm embarrassed to go home.

CARSON HERRON, AN AMERICAN CLUB PROFESSIONAL, ON HIS FIRST-ROUND PERFORMANCE IN THE 1963 US OPEN AT THE COUNTRY CLUB IN BROOKLINE

Who plays golf any more? I've gone in for gambling now. At the tables I only lose my money. On the course I lose my mind.

JACKIE MILES, AMERICAN COMIC

I'll hustle anyone for a dollar – or a dime!

LEE TREVINO, GOLF HUSTLER TURNED MAJOR CHAMPIONSHIP WINNER

Hey David! You better play better than this if you wanna get paid.

AMERICAN FAN TO DAVID DUVAL AT THE RYDER CUP AT BROOKLINE IN 1999. BEFORE THE MATCH, DUVAL, AMONG OTHERS, HAD SUGGESTED THAT PERHAPS THE PLAYERS SHOULD RECEIVE PAYMENT FOR PLAYING.

I love it. I still think that we should have a say in the way charity money is directed, but I love this week anyway.

DAVID DUVAL, A MEMBER OF THE WINNING AMERICAN RYDER CUP TEAM IN 1999

The Power Game

Golf is a game kings and presidents play when they get tired of running countries.

    CHARLES PRICE

Put your fanny into the ball, Mr President.

    SAM SNEAD TO PRESIDENT DWIGHT D. EISENHOWER AT A PRO-AM EVENT

As General Eisenhower discovered, it is easier to end the Cold War or stamp out poverty than to master this devilish pastime.

    JAMES RESTON, AMERICAN JOURNALIST

We have 51 golf courses in Palm Springs. He [President Gerald Ford] never decides which course he will play until after the first tee shot.

    BOB HOPE

I know I'm getting better at golf because I'm hitting fewer spectators.

GERALD FORD

It does look like a very good exercise. But I wonder what is the little white ball for?

ULYSSES S. GRANT, US PRESIDENT, AFTER WATCHING A
NOVICE GOLFER SWING SEVERAL TIMES WITHOUT MAKING
CONTACT

I don't know of any game that makes you so ashamed of your profanity. It is a game full of moments of self-abasement, with only a few moments of self-exaltation. And we Americans, who are not celebrated for our modesty, may find such a game excellent training.

PRESIDENT TAFT

....

The fact that President Taft has chosen golf as the best out-of-door sport to keep him in good physical condition is responsible for an unprecedented congestion of players on the city's golf courses. The number of players on the Van Cortlandt and the Forest Park links have more than doubled since Taft's election and the publicity which has attended the President's almost daily play. In a way, it is pointed out, the fact is indicative that Americans are imitative in their patriotism, and diligently follow the examples set by the head of the Nation. Last year it used to be tennis, because that was President Roosevelt's hobby. Now the tennis courts are almost deserted, except for the habitual players. Many of this year's golf players are of an entirely different calibre.

TOM WHITE, CLUBHOUSE MANAGER OF THE VAN
CORTLANDT GOLF CLUB, 1909

I was playing once with the King of Samoa. I asked him what his handicap was. 'Six wives,' he said.

JACK REDMOND, AMERICAN TRICK-SHOT ARTIST

[The story] was probably dreamed up by some fool with a typewriter.

A BELEAGUERED BUCKINGHAM PALACE PRESS OFFICER, RESPONDING TO A STORY IN THE AMERICAN TABLOIDS WHICH CLAIMED THAT DIANA, PRINCESS OF WALES, HAD SCORED A HOLE-IN-ONE AT ROYAL TROON WHILE PLAYING A FRIENDLY FOUR-BALL WITH PRINCE CHARLES, PRINCESS ANNE AND PRINCE ANDREW IN 1982!

How do you do, Mr Prime Minister – ever shake hands with a Mexican before?

LEE TREVINO, ON MEETING EDWARD HEATH, THE FORMER PRIME MINISTER OF GREAT BRITAIN, IN 1978

Playing the game, I have learned the meaning of humility. It has given me an understanding of the futility of human effort.

ABBA EBAN, FORMER ISRAELI AMBASSADOR

If I had my way, any man guilty of golf would be ineligible for any public office in the United States, and the families of the breed would be shipped off to the white slave corrals of the Argentine.

H. L. MENCKEN, AMERICAN JOURNALIST

I did not see the sense in chasing a little white ball around a field.

PRESIDENT CALVIN COOLIDGE, ON WHY HE NEVER PLAYED GOLF

Here you are, the greatest golfer in the world, being introduced by the worst one.

JAMES WALKER, MAYOR OF NEW YORK, AT A CITY HALL CEREMONY HONOURING BOBBY JONES'S 'GRAND SLAM' IN 1930

Yes, a lot more people beat me now.

DWIGHT D. EISENHOWER, ASKED IF HIS GAME HAD CHANGED SINCE LEAVING THE WHITE HOUSE

Vice-President Spiro Agnew can't cheat on his score – because all you have to do is look back down the fairway and count the wounded.

BOB HOPE

I play little golf now since a crowd of yobs prevented my playing here [at Lossiemouth] but I shall be so delighted to see you that I shall take up that challenge of yours. My handicap used to be seven but I must now be something like 100. I shall take down a friend or two and we shall have a jolly day of it.

RAMSAY MACDONALD, PRIME MINISTER OF GREAT BRITAIN, REPLYING TO AN INVITATION FOR A GAME OF GOLF

Golf is the only game where the worst player gets the best of it. He obtains more out of it as regards both exercise and enjoyment, for the good player gets worried over the slightest mistake, whereas the poor player makes too many mistakes to worry over them.

DAVID LLOYD GEORGE, PRIME MINISTER OF GREAT BRITAIN, WHO WAS ONCE DEBAGGED AT WALTON HEATH BY SUFFRAGETTES

There is no reason ... why golf should not be begun as soon as one can walk and continued as long as one can walk.

A. J. BALFOUR, PRIME MINISTER OF GREAT BRITAIN AND LIFE-LONG GOLF ADDICT

Golf always makes me so damned angry.

KING GEORGE V

....

Here, Eddie, hold the flag while I putt out.

WALTER HAGEN'S INFORMAL REQUEST TO EDWARD, PRINCE OF WALES (LATER KING EDWARD VIII)

....

I like going there for golf. America is one vast golf course today.

EDWARD, DUKE OF WINDSOR (FORMERLY KING EDWARD VIII) IN THE 1950S

Golf seems to me an arduous way to go for a walk. I prefer to take the dogs out.

HRH PRINCESS ANNE

Whenever I play with him, I usually try to make it a foursome – Ford, me, a paramedic and a faith healer.

BOB HOPE ON THE GOLFING PROWESS OF FORMER US PRESIDENT, GERALD FORD

He told me he was having a meeting with some Bishops, but that he had managed to escape for a while to congratulate me. The King said that they were all watching me on television and were all very nervous. I also had a call from Spain's Prime Minister, José Maria Aznar, who was heading for a meeting with President Clinton in Washington. He asked me whether he could tell the President that his friend 'Chema' had beaten his friend Greg, and of course I said yes. Then I heard that the President asked our Prime Minister if he could organize a game with me. If we play in the States I will ask for some strokes – just in case!

JOSÉ MARIA OLAZABAL, ON THE PHONE CALLS HE RECEIVED AT HIS RENTED AUGUSTA HOME SHORTLY AFTER WINNING THE 1999 US MASTERS

Golf obviously provides one of our best forms of healthful exercise accompanied by good fellowship and companionship.

DWIGHT D. EISENHOWER

President Eisenhower has given up golf for painting. It takes fewer strokes.

BOB HOPE

Augusta is the course 'Ike' Eisenhower usually plays on. That's proof enough for me that he is a man with good taste.

JIMMY DEMARET

I ran out of balls before I could complete eighteen holes!

JESSE VENTURA, GOVERNOR OF MINNESOTA AND US
PRESIDENTIAL CANDIDATE, DESCRIBING A VISIT TO
CARNOUSTIE

Playing golf is like chasing a quinine pill around a cow pasture.

WINSTON CHURCHILL, ON THE FRUSTRATION OF PLAYING
THE GAME

Once upon a time I went down to Sandwich with the Aga Khan and J. H. Taylor; His Highness was not in form, and was getting depressed. It was summer, and the ground was hard, and as we approached the last green the Aga Khan hit his ball hard on the top and accordingly was stricken with sadness. Suddenly I heard Taylor's voice saying, 'Really, your Highness, what is the use of my dinning into your ears to pitch the ball up to the hole when these run-up shots come so naturally to you?' The next day the Aga Khan played very well, and I could not help thinking that Taylor's words of encouragement on the previous day had something to do with it.

LORD CASTLEROSS, 1934

The PGA? Well, that just goes to show you that no matter how closely you try and keep in touch with what's happening in Washington, the moment you turn your back the government has created another agency.

LORD HALIFAX, FORMER BRITISH AMBASSADOR TO THE
UNITED STATES, ON THE FLEDGELING PROFESSIONAL
GOLFERS ASSOCIATION, 1938

If I swung the gavel like I swung a golf club, the nation would be in a hell of a mess.

TIP O'NEILL, WHILE HE WAS SPEAKER OF THE US HOUSE OF REPRESENTATIVES

In golf, you keep your head down and follow through. In the vice-presidency, you keep your head up and follow through. It's a big difference.

DAN QUAYLE, FORMER US VICE-PRESIDENT AND LOW-HANDICAP GOLFER

You get to know more of the character of a man in a round of golf than in six months of political experience.

DAVID LLOYD GEORGE

One lesson you'd better learn if you want to be in politics is that you never go out on a golf course and beat the President.

LYNDON B. JOHNSON

Booverman, on the contrary, had been hailed in his first years as a coming champion. With three holes eliminated, he could turn in a card distinguished for its fours and threes; but unfortunately these sad lapses inevitably occurred. As Booverman himself admitted, his appearance on the golf links was the signal for the capricious imps of chance who stir up politicians to indiscreet truths and keep the Balkan pot of discord bubbling, to forsake immediately these prime duties, and enjoy a little relaxation at his expense.

OWEN JOHNSON, *EVEN THREES*, 1912

Golf is to me what his Sabine farm was to Horace – a solace and an inspiration.

RAMSAY MACDONALD, PRIME MINISTER OF GREAT BRITAIN

The problem with golf is I have to deal with a humiliation factor.

GEORGE BUSH, FORMER PRESIDENT OF THE UNITED STATES

No one has mastered golf until he has realized that his good shots are accidents and his bad shots, good exercise.

EUGENE BLACK, AMERICAN GOVERNMENT OFFICIAL

By the time you get dressed, drive out there, play 18 holes and come home, you've blown seven hours. There are better things you can do with your time.

RICHARD NIXON

It is true that my predecessor did not object, as I do, to pictures of one's golf skill in action. But neither, on the other hand, did he ever bean a Secret Serviceman.

JOHN F. KENNEDY, ON HIS LACK OF ACCURACY OFF THE TEE

Yes, I have a higher approval rating than President Clinton.

DOTTIE PEPPER, AMERICAN SOLHEIM CUP PROFESSIONAL,
RESPONDING TO HER 82% APPROVAL RATING FOR HER
ALLEGEDLY CONTROVERSIAL BEHAVIOUR IN THE 1998 MATCH

Dan would rather play golf than have sex any day.

MARILYN QUAYLE, WIFE OF FORMER VICE-PRESIDENT, DAN

Bob [Hope] says I have made golf a combat and contact sport.

GERALD FORD

My golf-loving friend Bob Hope asked me what my handicap was, so I told him – the Congress.

RONALD REAGAN, 1982

Did you read that Arnold Palmer has been talking about the governorship of Pennsylvania? Man, I think that hip injury must be moving up to his head.

DAVE MARR, ON ARNIE'S POLITICAL ASPIRATIONS, 1968

[Bill Clinton] told me he caddied in the same group with me in the Hot Springs [Arkansas] Open. That's why I voted for him, because he was my caddie.

TOMMY BOLT

With all the Korean people, I express my joy over your victory. You are a hero of this era and our hope.

PRESIDENT KIM DAE-JUNG, SENDING HIS
CONGRATULATIONS TO HIS COUNTRYWOMAN SE RI PAK ON
WINNING THE US WOMEN'S OPEN, 1998

And don't come back without the Cup.

PRESIDENT GEORGE BUSH, STRESSING THE IMPORTANCE OF
VICTORY TO THE AMERICAN RYDER CUP TEAM BEFORE
THEIR DEPARTURE FOR THE UK IN 1989

Rules of the Game

Golf requires only a few simple Rules and Regulations to guide the players in the true nature of its sporting appeal. The spirit of the game is its own referee.

ROBERT HARRIS, *SIXTY YEARS OF GOLF*, 1953

....

At first sight golf would seem to require few laws; the manner of play is simple and there are but two contracting parties. From here to there the ball must go, propelled by the rival forces, the side being victorious which make the goal in fewer strokes than the enemy. Beyond this straightforward declaration of procedure there would seem to be no necessity for the law. The pity of golf today is that men play entirely to win and are afraid that they may be defrauded by some inequality of penalty from gaining the end of their desire. It would be happier for golf if we would only remember that the true good is in the playing, not in the winning.

JOHN LOW, *THE GOLFER'S HANDBOOK*, 1905

....

Local rules in golf – a set of regulations that are ignored by players on a specific course rather than by golfers as a whole.

ROY McKIE, BRITISH AUTHOR

The uglier a man's legs are, the better he plays golf. It is almost a law.

H. G. WELLS

Harassed secretaries, who from time to time are called to arbitrate upon such knotty problems, go in danger of their lives, and when two disputants walk into his office at the close of a particularly bitter round before the 19th, each firmly gripping their blasters [sand wedges] and demanding equal justice, the inoffensive servant of the club will require the courage of a Canute, the wisdom of a Solomon, and the effrontery of a Dr Johnson.

H. MacNEILE DIXON, GOLF AND HOW, 1944

In a generation or two, or maybe sooner, young golfers of true sporting instinct will wonder why all this handling of the ball is necessary. It will seem to them that the game is not as good as it might be.

ROBERT HARRIS, ON BEING ABLE TO MARK THE BALL ON THE GREENS, SIXTY YEARS OF GOLF, 1953

Golf: the only game in the world in which a precise knowledge of the rules can earn one a reputation for bad sportsmanship.

PATRICK CAMPBELL

I think most of the rules of golf stink.

CHI CHI RODRIGUEZ

I want a ruling. I want to know which club to hit this guy with.

It is a law of nature that everybody plays a hole badly when playing through.

In competition, during gunfire or while bombs are falling, players may take cover without penalty for ceasing play. The positions of known delayed-reaction bombs are marked by red flags at a reasonably, but not guaranteed, safe distance therefrom … A ball moved by enemy action may be replaced, or if lost or 'destroyed' a ball may be dropped not nearer the hole without penalty. A player whose stroke is affected by the simultaneous explosion of a bomb may play another ball from the same place. Penalty, one stroke.

What's the penalty for killing a photographer – one stroke or two?

The golfer is an honest man.

Golf is a game where the ball lies poorly, and the players well.

ANON.

I've always had three rules for playing well on the tour: no push-ups, no swimming and no sex after Wednesday.

SAM SNEAD

You mustn't blow your nose when your partner is addressing the ball.

HENRY LONGHURST

The entire handbook can be reduced to three rules. One: you do not touch your ball from the time you tee it up to the moment you pick it out of the hole. Two: don't bend over when you are in the rough. Three: when you are in the woods, keep clapping your hands.

CHARLES PRICE, RESPECTED AMERICAN GOLF WRITER

The challenger was about to play his fourth shot towards the green when across his line of play casually wandered a cow and calf, stopping at this moment to browse upon the succulent herbage so bountifully, though possibly carelessly, provided by Mother Earth at this particular place. About to swing, he stopped and asked permission from his opponent to move the object, as laid down quite clearly in Rule 11. The reply came: 'The cow alone but not her offspring – it is still growing.'

H. MACNEILE DIXON, *GOLF AND HOW,* 1944

The only times you touch the ball with your hand are when you tee it up and when you pick it out of the cup. The hell with television towers and cables and burrowing animals and the thousand and one things that are referred to as 'not part of the golf course'. If you hit the ball off the fairway, you play it from there.

KEN VENTURI, 1964 US OPEN CHAMPION

Rule One: Whenever a spectator seeks out a really good vantage point and settles down on shooting stick or canvas chair, the tallest and fattest golf watcher on the course will take up station directly in front.

PETER DOBEREINER

Golf was invented by some Scotsman who hit a ball, with a stick, into a hole in the ground. The game today is exactly the same, except that it now takes some ninety-odd pages of small type to ensure that the ball is hit with the stick into the hole in the ground without cheating.

A. S. GRAHAM

Players should pick up bomb and shell splinters from the fairways in order to save damage to the mowers.

LOCAL RULE, RYE GOLF CLUB, BRITAIN, 1940

The rules are simple and easily understood by anyone who has once seen the game, but to the totally uninitiated they appear to be hopelessly unintelligible.

JOHN GILMER SPEED, *THE LADIES JOURNAL*, 1894

I have always believed there are far too many rules in golf. For me, if you cannot write them all on the back of a matchbox then something is wrong.

HENRY LONGHURST

As an orthodox golfer, born and bred in the true faith north of the Tweed, though now unhappily chained to London, I have often been surprised and pained, not so much at the Englishman's madness for the game, as at the manner of it. To him we owe, amongst other things, the perplexing and uncalled-for mutilation of the ancient rules to suit the exigencies of local greens.

GARDEN G. SMITH, IN A LETTER TO THE EDITOR OF *GOLF* MAGAZINE, COMPLAINING ABOUT THE SURFEIT OF LOCAL RULES AT ENGLISH GOLF COURSES, 1896

There is no surer or more painful way to learn a rule than to be penalized once for breaking it.

TOM WATSON

I'll take the two-stroke penalty, but I'll be damned if I'll play it where it lays.

ELAINE JOHNSON, CANADIAN AMATEUR GOLFER, AFTER THE BALL SHE HIT ENDED UP IN HER OWN BRA, *GOLF DIGEST*, 1983

There are more 'Don'ts' in golf than there are in any other avocation in life.

ARNOLD HAULTAIN, *THE MYSTERY OF GOLF*, 1910

A small ball has to be hit by a variety of clubs over grass country of uneven contour into a small hole in the ground. Difficulties in the shape of sand holes, ditches, streams, bushes and other natural objects are met in the journey from starting point to hole. These are surmounted by skilful shots or bypassed by manoeuvre. There are certain penalties and forfeits for inefficient play or an unlucky lie of the ball. These penalties have been exacted for centuries and found to operate with all fairness.

ROBERT HARRIS, TOP ENGLISH AMATEUR, 1926

St Andrews has ever been a law unto itself in golf.

CHARLES B. MACDONALD, MEMBER OF THE USGA
COMMITTEE ON THE RULES OF GOLF, 1898

If the player has succeeded in throwing or pushing his ball into a hole, his opponent must wait until he has succeeded in spooning it out before he begins to play. Obedience to this rule obviates any dispute as to the order in which a man's points are to be made.

THE PHILADELPHIA TIMES, 1889

In golf, a player can step and mar the line of his adversary's putt. A player can also hit his adversary or his caddie intentionally with his ball and claim the hole — but it isn't usually done.

CHARLES B. MACDONALD, MEMBER OF THE USGA
COMMITTEE ON THE RULES OF GOLF, 1898

On the fair green, grass or driving course, stones, bones or any break club, within a club length of the ball, may be removed.

THE SECOND RULE OF GOLF ADOPTED BY THE HONOURABLE
COMPANY OF EDINBURGH GOLFERS IN 1839

You might as well praise a man for not robbing a bank as to praise him for playing by the rules.

BOBBY JONES

If he takes the option of dropping behind the point where the ball rests, keeping in line with the pin, his nearest drop is Honolulu.

JIMMY DEMARET, OFFERING HIS OPINION ON WHERE
ARNOLD PALMER COULD DROP AFTER MISSING THE GREEN
ON THE 17TH HOLE AT PEBBLE BEACH, 1964

On the first tee you drop the ball over your left shoulder.

JIMMY DEMARET, ON THE DIFFICULTY OF ONE PARTICULAR
COURSE

It is the general testimony of golf authorities that there is nothing that so strains a person's integrity as the obeying of this rule. The temptation to touch the ball with the foot and put it into a better position for a good stroke is said to be too great for some players to resist. These authorities also agree in saying that a man who once yields to this temptation is irretrievably lost, and that his capacity to be honest in golf is as hopelessly gone as the power of a sheep-killing dog to stop taking his mutton on the hoof. These authorities recommend not betting heavily with such offenders, but in other regards not to pay any attention to their play.

JOHN GILMER SPEED, *THE LADIES JOURNAL,* 1894

If a ball comes to rest in dangerous proximity to a hippopotamus or crocodile, another ball may be dropped at a safe distance, no nearer the hole, without penalty.

LOCAL RULE AT NYANZA GOLF CLUB, BRITISH EAST AFRICA, 1952

One of these days I'm going to write a book on drops. That ought to sell. The shot's become more popular than putting.

JIMMY DEMARET, ON A BOOK WHICH HE NEVER DID WRITE, 1952

Right up to the late 1940s, there were no discs to mark your ball on the green. If you did not want to putt out, pros would get out a tee and mark a single line in the grass, away from the ball at right angles to the hole so it would be very easy to replace the ball at the other end of the mark if this gave any advantage. Of course by the end of the day, the grass round the hole would be etched with a mass of lines. Nowadays if you even touch the surface with anything other than a disc you can be penalized, because you are deemed to be testing the condition of the green.

MAX FAULKNER, 1951 BRITISH OPEN CHAMPION

St Andrews, the Home of Golf

I wish that every man who plays golf should play at St Andrews once.

GENE SARAZEN

If I had ever been set down in any one place and told I was to play there, and nowhere else, for the rest of my life, I should have chosen the Old Course.

BOBBY JONES, LEGENDARY GOLFER, ON BEING PRESENTED WITH THE FREEDOM OF ST ANDREWS IN 1958

Despite its almost mythical reputation, the Old Course is not universally liked by everyone. The ancient links offer pleasure and pain in equal measure – often, all in the space of one hole. Frequently frustrating as it is, many of the world's top golfers have left St Andrews asking what all the fuss is about, while others enthuse about its challenge until their dying day. Of course there are some who miss the point altogether. They are usually the ones who berate the venerable links for having too many blind shots, no buggy paths and not enough island greens!

A. J. DALCONEN, *GOLF: THE HISTORY OF THE ROYAL & ANCIENT GAME*, 1995

We feel drawn to Mr Jones by ties of affection and personal regard of a particularly cordial nature, and we know that he himself has declared his own enduring affection for this place and for its people. Like many cordial and enduring partnerships it was not, I think, a case of love at first sight. I believe that, for his part, the first impressions that he formed of the Old Course were something less than favourable. But back he came in 1930 to master the intricacies of golf at St Andrews, as they have never been mastered before, even by our giants of the nineteenth century, and to win his way, not only to the Open Championship, but into the hearts of St Andrews people.

PROVOST ROBERT LEONARD OF ST ANDREWS, OUTLINING THE REASONS WHY BOBBY JONES WAS GIVEN THE FREEDOM OF THE CITY IN 1958

A shepherd tending his sheep would chance upon a round pebble. He would strike it away, for it is inevitable that a man with a stick in his hand should aim a blow at any loose object lying in his path as that he should breathe ... Feeding his sheep on the links, perhaps those of St Andrews, he rolled one of these stones into a rabbit scrape. 'Marry,' he quoth, 'I could not do that if I tried ...'

SIR WALTER SIMPSON, SPECULATING ON HOW GOLF BEGAN AT ST ANDREWS, *THE ART OF GOLF*, 1887

Would you like to see a city given over soul and body to a tyrannizing game? If you would there's little need to be a rover, for St Andrews is the abject city's name.

ANON?

Rich and poor alike are smitten by the fever
Their business and religion is to play;
And a man is scarcely deemed a true believer,
Unless he goes at least a round a day.

R. F. MURRAY, 1885

Golf without St Andrews would be almost as intolerable as St Andrews without Golf. Here the children make their entrance into the world, not with silver spoons in their mouths, but with diminutive golf-clubs in their hands. Here the Champion is as much a hero as the greatest general who ever returned in triumph from the wars. Here, in short, is an asylum for golfing maniacs and the happy hunting-ground of the duffer, who, armed with a rusty cleek, sallies forth to mutilate the harmless turf.

ROBERT BARCLAY, *A BATCH OF GOLFING PAPERS*, 1892

Until you play it, St Andrews looks like the sort of real estate you couldn't give away.

SAM SNEAD

As the traveller approaches St Andrews everything indicates that Golf is the business of the place.

ANON.

The Road Hole, the 17th, is the most famous and infamous hole. As a planner and builder of golf holes world-wide, I have no hesitation in allowing that if one built such a hole today you would be sued for incompetence.

PETER THOMPSON, AUSTRALIAN PROFESSIONAL TURNED GOLF COURSE ARCHITECT

St Andrews: a course that tells you no lies.

ANDREW KIRKALDY, OLD-TIME SCOTTISH PROFESSIONAL, 1891

He made golf his life more thoroughly than any man we know. Sutherland was not much of a player himself, but he approached immortality on two counts. The first was that he became the first steward [referee] at a golf match in history. Secondly, when the bunker at the 15th, a few yards beyond the Cottage Bunker, was named after him, because he spent more time in it than he did in his home.

ROBERT CHAMBERS, ON R&A STALWART THE DUKE OF SUTHERLAND, 1872

The greatest of his day has died. They may toll the bells and shut up the shops in St Andrews, for their greatest is gone.

THE DUKE OF SUTHERLAND, ON THE DEATH OF GOLF'S FIRST PROFESSIONAL, ALLAN ROBERTSON, 1859

[St Andrews ...] the city of magnificent obsession.

R. F. MURRAY, BRITISH SPORTS JOURNALIST, 1950

This place is the very soul of golf. You have to use your imagination. I always enjoy being here.

José Maria Olazabal

The Old Course has for a century and a half been regarded as the sceptre of the game; it is the symbol par excellence of real golf. It became and still is the Mecca of the golf-playing world both from tradition and the sporting appeal of its natural and accidental lay-out.

Robert Harris, *Sixty Years of Golf*, 1953

It is disgraceful of the railway people bringing a parcel of uneducated brutes down here when they knew a real match was going on.

The Duke of Sutherland, on a group of rowdy visitors arriving in St Andrews from nearby Dundee in 1877. Unaware there was an important professional match in progress, they streamed over the links, setting up picnics and the like. Typically, Sutherland strode forward, club in hand, waving them frantically off the course.

What train?

Joyce Wethered, showing her powers of concentration during her famous match with Glenna Collett in the 1929 British Ladies Championship. As she stood on the 16th tee, a steam train passed by while she was about to putt. Without a flicker she holed out, and someone asked her whether the train had put her off. This was her answer.

Nothing can be more certain than that the exercise of golf is preferred to all others at St Andrews, and generally considered as a sort of necessary of life.

PART OF A LEGAL PLEA BY THE INHABITANTS OF ST ANDREWS, c 1800

....

The reason the Road Hole at St Andrews is the greatest par four in the world is because it's a par five.

BEN CRENSHAW, FORMER US MASTERS CHAMPION AND GOLF HISTORIAN

....

[The] natives [of St Andrews] have a pleasure of their own which is as much the staple of the place as old colleges and churches are. This is golfing which is here not a mere pastime, but a business and a passion, and has for ages been so, owing probably to their admirable links. There is a pretty large set who do nothing else, who begin in the morning and stop only for dinner; and who, after practising the game in the sea breeze, discuss it all night.

LORD COCKBURN, 1874

Sir David Moncrieffe backs his life against the life of John Whyte-Melville for a new Silver Club, as a present to the St Andrews Golf Club (Society of Golfers). The price of the club to be paid by the survivor.

THE R&A WAGERS BOOK, 1819, WHERE MEMBERS PLAYED FOR UNUSUALLY HIGH STAKES!

He was the best golfer who ever addressed himself to a ball.

ROBERT CLARK, ON THE LEGENDARY YOUNG TOM MORRIS OF ST ANDREWS, 1880

He was far more useful to me than a club. Without his help I doubt if I could have won it. It amazed me the way he just put the club in my hand.

TONY LEMA, WINNER OF THE 1964 OPEN CHAMPIONSHIP AT ST ANDREWS, ON HIS LOCAL CADDIE, TIP ANDERSON

Those links which possess no hazards are considered inferior to those on which they plentifully occur, and it may be stated that on difficult links it requires more real golfing science to avoid driving balls into, than out of, hazards. Hazards consist of sand-pits [bunkers], gorse or whin bushes, cad-roads, long grass, water, etc; as a ball must, with certain exceptions, be played where it lies, the avoidance of hazards constitutes much of the superiority of an excellent player.

ROBERT CHAMBERS, ON ST ANDREWS, 1860

The admitted supremacy of St Andrews as a golfing centre may in various ways be accounted for; socially and otherwise the place has always been a pleasant one.

ROBERT CLARK, *THE ROYAL & ANCIENT GAME OF GOLF*, 1875

The majority of the fairways at St Andrews do resemble a green moonscape and rarely, if ever, offer the golfer a flat lie. Apart from the 1st and 18th holes, St Andrews is also plagued with bunkers. As if getting out of them were not difficult enough, they all have evocative names like 'Principal's Nose', 'Lion's

Mouth', 'Coffins' and 'Grave'. Never uniform, they vary in size and shape from a large dustbin lid to those like 'Hell' bunker which is big enough to merit its own par.

A. J. Dalconen, *Golf: The History of the Royal & Ancient Game*, 1995

To the material prosperity of the City the Links are very vital indeed. The questions at issue affect, directly or indirectly, every St Andrews proprietor and householder, whether they are golfers or not. The present course is already far too restricted for the demands made upon it in the summer. With the well deserved and rapidly increasing popularity of the game, it may be safely stated that two or even three courses would be none too many for the Metropolis of golf.

Dr Hay Fleming, local historian, campaigning for more golf courses at St Andrews, 1888

Go back for it yersel. I'm paid to carry your bag – not to fetch and carry!

A St Andrews caddie who was asked by an American visitor to pick up his cigar case left on the previous tee, *Golf Monthly*, 1955

[They] stood disloyally near the tee ...

Sir Guy Campell, describing the driving-in ceremony of the newly elected captain of the R&A, Edward, Duke of Windsor, 1922. At St Andrews, the fortunate caddie who collects the ball is presented with a silver sovereign. Unfortunately, the Duke had a reputation for topping the ball, which is what he did.

The early part of the match went greatly in favour of the Dunns, whose play was magnificent. Their driving, in fact, completely overpowered their opponents. They went sweeping over hazards which the St Andrews men had to play short of.

H. THOMAS PETER, DESCRIBING A £400 CHALLENGE
MATCH AT NORTH BERWICK IN 1849 BETWEEN THE
CHAMPIONS OF ST ANDREWS, TOM MORRIS AND ALLAN
ROBERTSON, AND THE DUNN BROTHERS OF MUSSELBURGH,
GOLFING REMINISCENCES OF AN OLD HAND, 1890

Maybe I am drunk! But I'll be sober by the morning and you'll still be a bad golfer!

ST ANDREWS CADDIE ON BEING FIRED FOR BEING DRUNK,
1920s

... [he was] one of those correctly fashioned and punctilious golfers whose stance was modelled on classic lines, whose drive, though it averaged only 25 yards over the hundred, was always a well-oiled and graceful exhibition of the Royal St Andrews swing. The left sole thrown up, the eyeballs bulging with the last muscular tension, the club carried back until the whole body was contorted into the first position of the traditional hoop snake preparing to descend a hill. He used the interlocking grip, carried a bag with a spoon driver, an aluminium cleek, had three abnormal putters, and wore one chamois glove with air holes on the back. He never accomplished the course in less than 85 and never exceeded 94, but, having aimed to set a correct example rather than to strive vulgarly for professional records, was always in a state of offensive optimism due to a complete sartorial satisfaction.

OWEN JOHNSON, *EVEN THREES*, 1912

St Andrews? I feel like I'm back visiting an old grandmother. She's crotchety and eccentric but also elegant. Anyone who doesn't fall in love with her has no imagination.

TONY LEMA, WINNER OF THE 1964 OPEN AT ST ANDREWS

Any golfer worth his salt has to cross the sea and try to win the British Open.

JACK NICKLAUS, ON WINNING THE 1970 OPEN AT ST ANDREWS

There's nothing wrong with the St Andrews course that a hundred bulldozers couldn't put right. The Old Course needs a dry clean and press.

ED FURGOL, FORMER US TOUR PROFESSIONAL

I don't have any particular affection for the turf, in a sacred sense. I played here in the Walker Cup and thought there were 15 blind holes and wasn't all that keen on the other three. Every round is the same here, I make two birdies and two bogeys. It's like Groundhog Day.

MARK JAMES, EUROPEAN RYDER CUP CAPTAIN, 1999

For history and tradition there is nowhere like it in the world but I don't think it's the fairest course. It doesn't require you to be incredibly accurate off the tee, and you can hit what you think is a good tee shot and it kicks into a bunker it is hard to get out of. Then you pitch on to a green ten feet from the flag and it can roll 30 yards away. It wouldn't be in my top 200 – in Fife!

LEE WESTWOOD

The golfer who does not take himself a caddie at St Andrews denies himself the wine of the country.

HERBERT WARREN WIND, AMERICAN GOLF WRITER

Shame on yer! Booing an' cheering like that ... Would ya do that in yon Kirk [church]!

TAM CHISHOLM, A LOCAL CADDY, ADDRESSING SOME ROWDY SPECTATORS DURING THE 1885 BRITISH OPEN AT ST ANDREWS

If I were you, I'd take the 9.40 train out of St Andrews.

ANDREW KIRKALDY, OCCASIONAL ST ANDREWS CADDIE, ON BEING ASKED BY A PARTICULARLY BAD GOLFER WHAT HE SHOULD DO NEXT

St Andrews, they say that thy glories are gone,
That thy streets are deserted, thy castles overthrown.
If thy glories be gone, they are only, methinks,
As it were, by enchantment, transferred to thy Links.

GEORGE FULLERTON CARNEGIE OF PITARROW, 1813

The course needs a rest on Sundays even if you do not!

OLD TOM MORRIS, TO AMERICAN VISITORS WHO WERE UPSET THAT THE OLD COURSE WAS SHUT ON THE SABBATH, 1903

It's a great golf hole. It gives you a million options, not one of them worth a damn.

TOM KITE, DESCRIBING THE PAR-FOUR 13TH AT ST ANDREWS, 1990

I hate its arrogant lumps and bumps and the times you must play shots with one leg up in the air.

NEIL COLES, FORMER BRITISH RYDER CUP GOLFER, ON HIS DISLIKE FOR LINKS-TYPE GOLF AT ST ANDREWS, 1984

I should have played that hole in an ambulance.

ARNOLD PALMER, AFTER TAKING TEN AT THE 17TH HOLE DURING THE 1960 OPEN AT ST ANDREWS

It finds you out. If there is one part of your game not right, no matter how you try to hide it – to protect it – the Old Course will find it during the championship.

PETER THOMSON, LEGENDARY AUSTRALIAN PROFESSIONAL

The problems do not stop at the greens. With double greens on the majority of holes, it becomes a constant source of embarrassment to anyone playing St Andrews for the first time to putt out within the shadow of the other flag. Excuses like 'I was aiming at the wrong hole' are usually treated with the contempt they deserve.

A. J. DALCONEN, *GOLF: THE HISTORY OF THE ROYAL & ANCIENT GAME*, 1995

The 17th hole, or 'Station Master's Garden', comes at the right place in a needle match. This is a nerve tester in its play from start to finish. No player ever stands on the tee here facing the black sheds without having to suppress a small tremor. It takes years of tolerance and failure to make modern golfers understand this is a golf hole. It is reviled, scoffed at once in a way, then it comes to be feared, cursed with vehemence as being stupid and unfair, but golfers who have played it, in course of time learn all about it. Those who haven't must see it to believe it.

ROBERT HARRIS, *SIXTY YEARS OF GOLF*, 1953

....

On leaving the 16th green we were all even. Both had a satisfactory drive over the Station Master's Garden going to the 17th green — one of the longest holes. Taylor played a fine second shot, his ball resting at the foot of the green. My second was away to the left behind the deep pot bunker. Some of my friends said, 'Pitch it over the bunker, Andrew.' I said, 'I dare not pitch this. If I do I'll put the ball in the road. Mr John Ball, Mr Harold Hilton and Mr John Low and many other leading amateurs of the day were standing by, weighing up the position. I noticed a little hollow to the right of the bunker and saw that if I played the shot properly I could cannon against the side and curl in towards the hole. But there was the risk of taking the wrong line and going into the bunker. 'Chance yer luck,' said John Herd, the uncle of Sandy Herd, who was my caddie. 'That's what I like to hear,' said I. 'No bunker-fright for me.' I chanced my luck and it came off. The shot was about twenty yards. I ran it up and the ball came beautifully round the bias of the ground and lay within two inches of the pin. 'Hard luck,' said somebody, thinking how near I was to holing out. But I had nothing to complain of with the ball lying where it did. The very ground seemed to shake with the clapping of the crowd ...

ANDREW KIRKALDY, DESCRIBING A CLOSE MATCH AGAINST THE LEGENDARY PUTTER J. H. TAYLOR AT ST ANDREWS IN 1902

....

As I walked that 130 yards to the green the cheers were deafening. I could not believe my fortune. There was another tremendous roar as my putt dropped. I took off my cap and put my head hard back to prevent the tears that were so very close. After 21 years the Old Course had opened up its heart to a competitor who has always had the utmost respect for its unique difficulties.

BOBBY LOCKE, ON WINNING THE OPEN CHAMPIONSHIP AT ST ANDREWS IN 1957

In my humble opinion, St Andrews is the most fascinating golf course I have ever played. There is always a way at St Andrews, although it is not always the obvious way, and in trying to find it, there is more to be learned on this British course than in playing a hundred ordinary American golf courses.

BOBBY JONES, 1930 GRAND SLAM WINNER

After one round I thought the Old Course was the worst I had ever known. On my second visit I played three rounds and ended by thinking it was quite a good course, after all. On the third occasion I played there for a week and ended up by concluding it was the most wonderful golf course in the world.

BOB GARDNER, DISTINGUISHED AMERICAN AMATEUR AND WALKER CUP CAPTAIN, 1926

Unhesitatingly, the Old Course of St Andrews is my favourite. I think it is the best and when I had to play a match of importance that was where I wanted to play it. St Andrews has character and features that you get nowhere else. What I like about it is that you may play a very good shot there and find yourself in a very bad place. That is a real game of golf.

GEORGE DUNCAN, 1920 OPEN CHAMPION

It is the best course in the world and there is none like it. I am more convinced of that the more I play it.

PETER THOMSON, FIVE TIMES OPEN CHAMPION

The visiting player must try to see the Old Course as it is ... an area of links land where golf has been played endlessly for nigh on a thousand years; whose original plan was shaped largely by nature and has stood the test of all that time. Nature's master plan has produced 18 holes that all possess their own character and individuality. That plan includes the simplest of ingredients; smooth, close-cropped turf, heather moorland and dense whin or gorse. A few big sandpits, such as Hell, the Cottage, and Shell bunkers which are far older than the course.

ERIC BROWN, SCOTTISH PROFESSIONAL AND FORMER RYDER CUP CAPTAIN, 1955

I have met strange opponents at golf; even stranger partners. I was once paired with an elderly man, till then unknown to me, now for ever memorable, who, after informing me, in confidence, that he was a familiar figure at St Andrews in the gutta-percha days, missed the object on the first tee, and, before I could intervene, took a second swish at the ball, which hit the ladies' tee-box and rebounded behind us into a gorse-bush. By weird methods we reached the sixth tee, which is high up, with a valley on each side. Off this he fell, to the left, while explaining the grandeurs of the hole ...

R. C. ROBERTSON-GLASGOW

Advice from the Golfing Gurus

All golfers, men and women, professional and amateur, are united by one thing – their desire to improve.

JUDY RANKIN

The teacher who helped me most was the one who told me the least.

JOHN JACOBS, NOTED GOLF COACH

If you want meat you go to the butcher's, and if you want your hair cut you go to the barber's. The same applies to golf. Don't listen to your playing companions, listen to the professionals.

JIMMY TARBUCK, BRITISH COMIC, ON TAKING ADVICE IN GOLF

Practice makes perfect is an old and very true saying. But to get the full benefit from practice you should try to work to a method or routine. It is often a waste of effort to go out on to the fairway with a huge bag of balls, take out your driver and slog away into the far distance until you are exhausted. Many times I have heard the complaint, 'I'm worse after practice', and that is why.

BERNARD HUNT, FORMER BRITISH RYDER CUP CAPTAIN

Finally, it always amuses me to consider that people who are learning to play golf have one big advantage over others in that their play sends them to parts of the country to which no one else ever goes!

DR DONALD SOPER, M.A.

Under an assumed name.

DUTCH HARRISON, US PROFESSIONAL OF THE 1950S, OFFERING SOUND ADVICE TO A PARTICULARLY POOR PLAYER WHO WANTED TO KNOW HOW TO PLAY A CHIP

I don't trust doctors. They are like golfers. Each one has a different answer to your problem.

SEVE BALLESTEROS

The chip shot from a bunker is like the lapidary's stroke on a diamond.

HENRY COTTON, EXPLAINING THE DELICATE NATURE OF BUNKER PLAY

To get an elementary grasp of the game of golf, a human must learn, by endless practice, a continuous and subtle series of highly unnatural movements, involving about 64 muscles, that result in a seemingly 'natural' swing, taking all of two seconds to begin and end.

ALISTAIR COOKE, BRITISH JOURNALIST AND BROADCASTER

Always fade a ball. You can't talk to a hook.

DAVE MARR

Those who think in terms of golf being a science unfortunately have tried to separate from each other the arms, head, shoulders, body, hips and legs. They turn the golfer into a worm that's been cut into bits, with each part wriggling every which way.

ERNEST JONES, BRITISH TEACHING PROFESSIONAL, 1949

If you can't outplay them, outwork them.

BEN HOGAN

To watch a first-class field drive off must convince everyone that a golf ball can be hit in many ways.

HENRY COTTON

Hitting my drives the right height for the day.

JOHN BALL, ON HOW HE WON THE 1890 OPEN
CHAMPIONSHIP AT WINDSWEPT PRESTWICK

I know that neither Taylor nor myself go by the books, yet between us we have won five out of the last six open championships.

HARRY VARDON, ASKED WHETHER HE EVER READ TEACHING
BOOKS, 1900

We have a tendency to be too deliberate. That is a real handicap. I am convinced that the average player would get more enjoyment and better scores if he abandoned the national habit of over-emphasizing the care necessary in every shot.

JEROME TRAVERS, 1915 US OPEN WINNER, ON THE
INCREASINGLY SLOW PLAY OF THE AMERICAN GOLFER, 1924

It is nothing new or original to say that golf is played one stroke at a time. But it took me many strokes to realize it.

BOBBY JONES

If you were assured that without imbibing any newfangled religion and regardless of all the new dietists and doctors who fill the human body full of parasites for the sake of destroying other parasites, you could not only add twenty years to the normal span of life, but secure in the present at least one good day out of seven by the simple process of swinging a golf club, would you not rush to the nearest golf links and begin to take lessons from the local professional?

A. J. WHIGHAM, AMERICAN ESSAYIST, 1910

Grip it and rip it.

ADVICE GIVEN TO BIG-HITTING JOHN DALY SHORTLY
BEFORE HIS VICTORY IN THE 1991 US PGA CHAMPIONSHIP
AT CROOKED STICK, INDIANA. IT LATER BECOME A FAMOUS
ADVERTISING SLOGAN ALL OVER THE WORLD.

It is an unwise pro that beats his only pupil.

GERALD BATCHELOR, BRITISH WRITER

Being left-handed is a big advantage. No one knows enough about your swing to mess you up with advice.

BOB CHARLES, STILL THE ONLY LEFT-HANDED GOLFER TO WIN THE BRITISH OPEN

....

The only thing you should force in a golf swing is the club back into the bag.

BYRON NELSON

....

You might as well expect a burglar to profit by the example of the Archbishop of Canterbury as to imagine that the ordinary indifferent player of golf will derive any benefit from the teachings of a British Champion.

THE UNNAMED AUTHOR OF *THE SECRET OF GOLF FOR OCCASIONAL PLAYERS*, DEPLORING THE RASH OF TEACHING BOOKS WRITTEN BY PROFESSIONAL GOLFERS, 1922

Men gravely devoting hours and money to a technique which so often they, apparently alone, do not know they can never master. The solemnity of their eternal failure is vastly comic. The perpetualness of their hope is nobly humorous.

R. C. ROBERTSON-GLASGOW

You can buy a country but you can't buy a golf swing. It's not on the shelf.

GENE SARAZEN

The pleasure derived from hitting the ball dead centre on the club is only comparable with one or two other pleasures that come to mind at the moment.

DINAH SHORE, AMERICAN ACTRESS AND TOURNAMENT
HOST

Not a week goes by without my learning something new about golf. That means, of course, that I was ignorant of eight things about golf two months ago. Extend that process back nearly twenty years and the result is an impressive accumulation of ignorance.

PETER DOBEREINER, BRITISH GOLF JOURNALIST

'Practice makes perfect,' they say. Of course, it doesn't. For the vast majority of golfers it merely consolidates imperfection.

HENRY LONGHURST

Golf is a science, the study of a lifetime, in which you can exhaust yourself but never your subject.

DAVID FORGAN

Long driving, if it be not the most deadly, is certainly the most dashing and fascinating part of the game; and of all others the principal difficulty of the Golfer to acquire, and his chief delight when he can manage it.

HENRY BROUGHAM FARNIE, AUTHOR OF THE FIRST EVER
GOLF INSTRUCTION BOOK IN 1857

Golf was never meant to be an exact science – it is an art form.

ANON.

Once your mind knows you've mis-aimed, your body gives up on making a good swing.

FRANK BEARD, AMERICAN PROFESSIONAL TURNED GOLF WRITER

Golf pro: an optimistic doctor who has a cure for dying.

JIM BISHOP, TOP AMERICAN COLUMNIST

There has been criticism that some professional golfers do not know how to teach. In defence of my competent colleagues in professional golf, I must point out that many pupils don't know how to take a lesson.

TOMMY ARMOUR

Never scold; if your partner is timid, it will make him nervous; if obstinate, he will sulk; if choleric, he will say unpleasant things or break his clubs. If you praise, do so sparingly and judiciously and without seeming to patronize, or his pride may take alarm; and give as little advice as possible unless you are asked for it. It is wonderful how much can be got out of even a bad player by good management and good feeling.

HORACE HUTCHINSON, *GOLF*, 1890

To sum up then, in what does the secret of good golf lie? Not in one thing, but in many. And in things so mysteriously conjoined, so incomprehensibly interwoven, as to baffle analysis.

ARNOLD HAULTAIN, *THE MYSTERY OF GOLF*, 1910

The general criticisms which are to be made of the average player's posture at address are that his feet are too far apart, his body is bent too much and his arms are extended too far.

BOBBY JONES

People are always telling me I should do one thing or another. I should change my grip or shorten my swing. I should practice more and goof around less. I shouldn't smile on Sunday. I should. I shouldn't. Frankly, I don't know why they worry. It's my life – and I don't worry.

FRED COUPLES

There is one essential only in the golf swing, the ball must be hit.

SIR WALTER SIMPSON, *THE ART OF GOLF*, 1887

Nobody ever swung the golf club too slowly.

BOBBY JONES

Six years are needed to make a golfer – three years to learn the game, then another three to unlearn all you have learned in the first three years. You might be a golfer when you arrive at this stage, but more likely you're just starting.

WALTER HAGEN

Can anyone name the 'greatest' atomic energy scientist? Yet, designing, engineering and constructing an atomic bomb is simple compared to trying to teach a fellow how to stop shanking.

TOMMY ARMOUR, DISCUSSING THE ATOMIC BOMB IN 1952

Lay off for three weeks and then quit for good.

It is this constant and undying hope for improvement that makes golf so exquisitely worth the playing.

BERNARD DARWIN, BRITISH WRITER

My golf swing is a bit like ironing a shirt. You get one side smoothed out, turn it over and there is a big wrinkle on the other side. Then you iron that one out, turn it over and there is yet another wrinkle.

TOM WATSON, ON HIS DECLINE, 1987

That's the worst swing I've ever heard.

PAT BROWNE, NATIONAL BLIND GOLF CHAMPION OF THE UNITED STATES, ABOUT ONE OF HIS PLAYING PARTNERS, 1988

The only difference between an amateur and a pro is that we call a shot that goes left-to-right a fade and an amateur calls it a slice.

PETER JACOBSEN, FORMER US RYDER CUP GOLFER

Good players have the power to think while they are competing. Most golfers are not thinking even when they believe they are. They are only worrying.

HARVEY PENICK

Nothing has changed since caveman days when some Neanderthal in plaid pants first picked up a club and tried to groove an inside-out path. We're all still looking for a repeating swing that works.

GLEN WAGGONER, AMERICAN WRITER

Golf is the perfection of an outdoor game. It implies walking at a steady pace without hurry or excitement, abundant, though not excessive, exercise to the arms, an education to the eye in estimating distances, and a training in graduating the amount of force to be used to send the ball the needful distance, and the niceties of the game afford an educational influence of great variety and high order.

ROYAL LEAMINGTON SPA ADVERTISER, 1897

Selecting a stroke is like selecting a wife. To each his own.

BEN HOGAN

The zone is the ability to give 110 per cent of your attention and your focus to the shot. When I'm on the tee, I'll see a divot in the fairway and try to run my ball over that divot – and succeed. That's the zone.

NICK PRICE, FORMER BRITISH OPEN AND PGA CHAMPION FROM ZIMBABWE

The first thing I learned was to swing hard, and never mind where the ball went.

JACK NICKLAUS, ON HOW HE STARTED LEARNING THE GAME

Your best shots in golf are your practice swing and the conceded putts. You'll never master the rest.

LORD ROBERTSON

Just hit the ball and go chase it.

JOHNNY MILLER, OFFERING ADVICE TO A BEGINNER, 1982

No man should attempt to play golf who has not good legs to run with and good arms to throw with, as well as a modicum of brain power to direct his play.

ALEXANDER MACFARLANE, *GLOBE-DEMOCRAT* NEWSPAPER, 1889

The right way to play golf is to go up and hit the bloody thing.

GEORGE DUNCAN, 1920 BRITISH OPEN CHAMPION

The art of teaching is a difficult one to master or understand; the genius is seldom a good instructor; the best players, just because they have found the game easy to learn, find it hard to teach.

MARK MCKENNA, *GOLF*, 1912

Any time a golfer hits a ball perfectly straight with a big club it is, in my view, a fluke.

JACK NICKLAUS

Golfers find it a very trying matter to turn at the waist, more particularly if they have a lot of waist to turn.

HARRY VARDON

Golf is like driving a car — as you get older, you get more careful.
SAM SNEAD

There are no bunkers in the air.
WALTER HAGEN, ON HIS PREFERENCE FOR HITTING THE
BALL HIGH, 1920

Give me a man with big hands, big feet and no brains and I will
make a golfer out of him.
WALTER HAGEN

In the actual playing of the game, the golfer cannot keep a great
amount of theory in mind and have any attention left to bestow
upon the ball.
JOHN D. DUNN, BRITISH PROFESSIONAL, 1916

You were hitting some shots out there that weren't making any
noise.
DAVE MARR, TO BRITISH GOLF AUTHOR GEORGE
PLIMPTON, AT THE BING CROSBY PRO-AM

Never hurry, never worry, and be sure to smell the flowers along
the way.
WALTER HAGEN AND HIS PHILOSOPHY OF GOLF

A strange mixture of frustration and joy, the game offers a limitless arena in which the full range of human emotions are
displayed. The challenge of mastering the sport also appears to

prove irresistible. For countless thousands each year, the sport becomes an obsession, with magazine articles detailing how to swing readily devoured and basic household chores neglected. It appears that once that first full-blooded drive has been smashed down the fairway, the golfing Rubicon has been well and truly crossed.

> A. J. Dalconen, *Golf: The History of the Royal & Ancient Game*, 1995

....

Not only is the stroke in golf an extremely difficult one, it is also an extremely complicated one, more especially the drive, in which its principles are accentuated. It is in fact a subtle combination of a swing and a hit; the 'hit' portion being deftly incorporated into the 'swing' portion just as the head of the club reaches the ball, yet without disturbing the regular rhythm of the motion. The whole body must turn on the pivot of the head of the right thigh bone working in the cotyloidal cavity of the os innominatum or pelvic bone, the head, right knee, and right foot remaining fixed with the eyes riveted on the ball. In the upward swing, the vertebral column rotates upon the head of the right femur, the right knee being fixed; and as the club-head nears the ball, the fulcrum is rapidly changed from the right to the left hip, the spine now rotating on the left thigh-bone, the left knee being fixed; and the velocity is accelerated by the arms and wrists, in order to add the force of the muscles to the weight of the body, thus gaining the greatest impetus possible.

> Arnold Haultain, *The Mystery of Golf*, 1910

....

The play from the ditch to the green was truly child's play. Many golfers dread putting, even the greatest. I have always loved putting and found it easy and immensely enjoyable. Equally I have always loved approach-play of all kinds. The first hole at Petersfield is an allegory of my golf. I was ridiculously obstinate about this hole. Sometimes I deliberately dared the Fates by putting down my best ball.

ARTHUR RAINSFORD, BRITISH WRITER, 1962

Keep on hitting it straight until the wee ball goes in the hole.

JAMES BRAID, FIVE TIMES WINNER OF THE BRITISH OPEN

I found out that all the important lessons of life are contained in the three rules for achieving a perfect golf swing: 1. Keep your head down. 2. Follow through. 3. Be born with money.

P. J. O'ROURKE, AMERICAN POLITICAL SATIRIST

As far as swing and techniques are concerned, I don't know diddly-squat. When I'm playing well, I don't even take aim.

FRED COUPLES

The reason the pro tells you to keep your head down is so you can't see him laughing.

PHYLLIS DILLER

Everybody has two swings – a beautiful practice swing and the choked-up one with which they hit the ball. So it wouldn't do either of us a damned bit of good to look at your practice swing.

ED FURGOL, FORMER US TOUR PROFESSIONAL

I've never lost a putting match to any of my pupils.
BILL FERGUSON, COACH TO IAN WOOSNAM AMONG OTHERS

The average golfer doesn't play golf; he attacks it.
JACKIE BURKE

Few learn golf in a lifetime.
GRANTLAND RICE, *AMERICAN GOLFER* MAGAZINE

I have a tip that can take five strokes off anyone's golf game. It is called an eraser.
ARNOLD PALMER, WITH SOME HELPFUL ADVICE FOR THE AMATEUR GOLFER

If you can hit the Ball straight down the middle,
If you can put each pitch upon the Green,
If you can solve that damned eternal riddle
Of playing every shot quite straight and clean,
If you can do these things I have suggested,
If you are really pleased when match is won,
If from the skies the 'Secret' you have wrested,
You may be scratch or plus one day, my Son.
ANON., 1899

There are three ways of learning golf: by study, which is the most wearisome; by imitation, which is the most fallacious; and by experience, which is the most bitter.
ROBERT BROWNING

What a shame to waste those great shots on the practice tee.

WALTER HAGEN

Occasionally, an enthusiastic golfer, driving from the 8th or 9th tee, may be seen to start immediately in headlong pursuit of a diverted ball, the swing of the club and the intuitive leap of the legs forward forming so continuous a movement that the main purpose of the game often becomes obscured to the mere spectator.

OWEN JOHNSON, *EVEN THREES*, 1912

Reverse every natural instinct you have and do just the opposite of what you are inclined to do and you will probably come very close to having a perfect golf swing.

BEN HOGAN

I've never had a coach. Most of the players can't seem to play without ringing up their coach every day. The way I look at it, if you can't sort out problems for yourself, then what's the point? Most people make everything far too complicated, in life as well as golf. You can pick up a club and just get on with it.

LAURA DAVIES, *THE ROUND OF MY LIFE*, 1998

I didn't need to finish college to know what golf was all about. All you need to know is to hit the ball, find it and hit it again until it disappears into the hole in the ground.

FUZZY ZOELLER

The only thing a golfer needs is more daylight.

BEN HOGAN

Paralysis by analysis.

BOBBY JONES, THE FIRST GOLFER TO EXPLAIN THE
PROBLEMS CAUSED BY OVER TEACHING

Never allow yourself to wander, and never play to the gallery. It is the steady game that brings the player to the fore.

J. H. TAYLOR, FIVE TIMES BRITISH OPEN CHAMPION

You don't hit anything on the backswing, so why rush it?

DOUG FORD, 1957 MASTERS CHAMPION

I have used a slow, deliberate swing all my career. Mainly because I have seen many golfers with small swing errors that become catastrophic because they swing at breakneck speed.

NANCY LOPEZ, *THE ROUND OF MY LIFE*, 1998

Most of the bad golf that is played is attributable to either a wrong method of holding the club or moving the head.

HARRY VARDON

Play for your fours and the threes will take care of themselves. It is from this willingness of the professional to take what the gods offer, as opposed to the amateur's tendency to strive for brilliant results, that the wide gap dividing their prowess has come about.

ROGER WETHERED

The follow through is not a cause, but an effect. It does not make you hit the ball correctly – it is merely the finest possible proof that you have hit the ball correctly.

JACK WHITE, 1904 OPEN CHAMPION, AUTHOR AND TEACHER

As kids, my brother and I were taught how to grip the club correctly and how to rip the ball. The only proviso he made was we had to finish the swing on our feet. When I eventually decided to play the game seriously, he told me if I was going to do it, then I should do it right, otherwise just play for fun. He never wanted me anywhere in between.

DAVIS LOVE III, DISCUSSING THE LESSONS HE LEARNED FROM HIS GOLF PROFESSIONAL FATHER, *THE ROUND OF MY LIFE*, 1998

In no other game must immense strength go hand in hand with extreme delicacy

ARNOLD HAULTAIN, *THE MYSTERY OF GOLF*, 1910

If the beginner can be brought to realize this simple truth about the difficulty of the game, he will have gained a great deal. One may then tell him that despite all the drudgery of painstaking practice that he will have to undergo, and the thousands of severe disappointments that he must inevitably endure, it does not follow that all the period of his studentship will be dull. The game will interest him and fascinate him almost as much after his first few lessons as it will do in many after-years.

JAMES BRAID, *HOW TO PLAY GOLF*, 1901

Let me give you one piece of general advice. Never, never comment on the fact that your opponent has got distance. Puzzled by your silence, long driver will try to outdistance even himself until, inevitably, he ends up out of bounds.

STEPHEN POTTER, *THE COMPLETE GOLF GAMESMANSHIP*, 1968

The 19th Hole

Now comes by far the most important part of the game, the playing of The 19th hole ... Thither the two players will adjourn, and over their whiskies and soda play the round all over again, hole by hole, stroke by stroke – that peach of a shot, my 11th [stroke] at the 4th, that bad luck I had hitting that misbegotten worm on the 13th green, and so on ... Then, having exhausted the topic, they will move to the billiards room and play a hundred up, or indulge in a frivolous game of darts, until, full of booze and bonhomie, the new member will return to the domestic hearth, there to regale his devoted wife with the same story once more which repetition can never render stale; and so fortified for the remainder of the week he can tackle his business cares with a light heart – until the next time.

H. MacNeile Dixon, *Golf and How*, 1944

Bibliography

Braid, James. *Advanced Golf.* London: Methuen, 1908.

Browning, Robert K. *A History of Golf.* London: J. M. Dent, 1955.

Campbell, Patrick. *How to Become a Scratch Golfer.* London: Anthony Blond, 1963.

Clark, Robert. Golf: *A Royal & Ancient Game.* Edinburgh: 1875.

Dalconen, A. J. *Golf: The History of the Royal & Ancient Game.* London: Salamander, 1995.

Darwin, Bernard. Permission by A. P. Watt Ltd on behalf of Ursula Mommens, Lady Darwin & Dr Paul Ashton.

Fitzpatrick, H. L. *Golf Don'ts.* New York: Doubleday Page, 1900.

Fletcher, Charles. *How to Play Bad Golf.* Los Angeles: privately printed, 1935.

Golf Monthly. IPC Publications, Stamford Street, London.

Golf World magazine (UK). EMAP Active, Peterborough.

Golf Illustrated/Golf Weekly. EMAP Active, Peterborough.

Harris, Robert. *Sixty Years of Golf.* Batchworth Press, 1953.

Hanks, Charles Stedman. *Hints to Golfers.* New York: Salem Press, 1903.

Hutchinson, Horace et al. *Golf.* London: Longmans Green, 1890.

Hutchinson, Horace. *Fifty Years of Golf.* Country Life, 1919.

Hyslop, Theodore. *Mental Handicaps in Golf.* Tindall & Cox, 1927.

Keeler, O. B. *The Bobby Jones Story.* Atlanta, Ga.: Tupper and Love, 1959.

Kenneth R. *The Mental Side of Golf: A Study of the Game*. London: Muller, 1955.

Kerr, J. *The Golf Book of East Lothian*. Edinburgh: Constable, 1896.

Longhurst, Henry. *Daily Telegraph*, London.

MacKenzie, Alister. *Golf Course Architecture*. London: Simpkin, Marshall, Hamilton & Kent, 1920.

Mappin, Major G. F. *The Golfing You*. Skeffington, 1948.

Ouimet, Francis. The Francis Ouimet Scholarship Fund Inc. Weston, Mass., USA.

Park, William. *The Game of Golf*. London: Longmans, 1899.

Potter, Stephen. *Golfmanship*. © Stephen Potter, 1968.

Price, Charles, ed. *The American Golfer* magazine.

Rice, Grantland. *The American Golfer* magazine.

Robertson, James K. *St Andrews*. Fife, Scotland: Citizen Office, 1967.

Simpson, Sir Walter. *The Art of Golf*. Edinburgh: Hamilton, 1887.

Sneddon, Richard. *The Golf Stream*. Philadelphia, Pa.: Dorrance, 1941.

Veteran, A. *The Secret of Golf for Occasional Players*. London: Methuen, 1922.

Wethered, Roger & Joyce. *Golf from Two Sides*. London: Longmans Green, 1922.

Wodehouse, P .G. Permission by A. P. Watt Ltd on behalf of Ursula Mommens, Lady Darwin & Dr Paul Ashton.

Photographic Acknowledgements

Jacket photograph supplied by the Dale Concannon Golf History Collection c/o The Phil Sheldon Golf Picture Library, 40 Manor Road, Barnet, Herts.

Index